It gives me a great deal of joy to [...]
A Hope and A Future. Don Wilton has live[...]
He brings us deep truth from God's Word in a way that can be practically applied and appropriate in our daily walk. We are living in a day of such superficiality and it is a breath of fresh air when God raises up the Don Wilton's of this world to give us the deeper truths of walking in victory. Read, be blessed, and then pass it on to friends!

—Dr. Johnny Hunt, SBC President and senior pastor of
First Baptist Church, Woodstock, Georgia

Don Wilton's personal ministry to my father has endeared himself to my entire family. The warmth of his shepherd's heart, his uncompromising proclamation of the gospel, his enthusiastic commitment to the church, and his love for God's Word . . . all combine to make him a wonderful pastor who has included our home in his house calls. God has surely used him also through the medium of television to help encourage many homebound saints, including my father, to keep their focus on *A Hope and A Future*.

—Anne Graham Lotz
Anne Graham Lotz, Bible teacher; author of
The Magnificent Obsession

Don is one of the most genuinely hopeful people I know—in fact I love to be around him because his Christianity is contagious. In *A Hope and A Future*, Don will inspire, encourage, and enable you to embrace the hope and the future that God has in store for you.

—Mac Brunson
pastor of First Baptist Church,
Jacksonville, Florida

For about twenty-five years, my husband and I have called Don and Karyn Wilton dear friends. They are lifelong partners in ministry who share similar callings and interests. They are friends who have multiplied our joys and divided our sorrows. There is no friend more encouraging to our personal lives or ministries than Don Wilton. He always gives us strength from the truths of God's Word. I am confident readers will find hope and encouragement from the biblical principles, practical applications, and necessary resolutions in this book. Reading *A Hope and A Future* is like entering into a conversation with an encouraging friend!

—Rhonda H. Kelley, Ph.D.
New Orleans Baptist Theological Seminary
President's Wife
Professor of Women's Ministry

Every person on the planet is looking for the same things. We all want to experience a hope and a future. In this book Don Wilton shows readers how those two things are more than just imaginary concepts; they are concrete realities. And as readers find themselves immersed in Don's personal experiences, inside perspectives, and powerful insights, they discover that a hope and a future are just the beginning of what God has in store.

—Ed Young
pastor of Fellowship Church in Grapevine, Texas and
author of *Outrageous, Contagious Joy*

I love my dad. We have always been best friends. Recently our relationship has grown even closer as partners in the gospel ministry. His words of encouragement over the phone, sipping coffee, on e-mail, and in his books have inspired my new ministry as a church planter in New Orleans. My city is filled with people who are searching for a hope and a future. I am excited to recommend this Christ-exalting book.

—Rob Wilton
pastor of Vintage Church
New Orleans, Louisiana

A
HOPE
AND A
FUTURE

A
HOPE
AND A
FUTURE

OVERCOMING
DISCOURAGEMENT

Don Wilton

PUBLISHING GROUP

NASHVILLE, TENNESSEE

978-0-8054-4555-8

Published by B&H Publishing Group,
Nashville, Tennessee

Dewey Decimal Classification: 234.2
Subject Heading: HOPE \ ENCOURAGEMENT \
BIBLE—INSPIRATION

1 2 3 4 5 6 7 8   •   13 12 11 10 09

This book is dedicated to a wonderful congregation of people at First Baptist Church, Spartanburg, South Carolina, and to The Encouraging Word Broadcast Ministry—who exist to "encourage complete and courageous living in Christ."

Acknowledgments

I am deeply grateful for the many opportunities God has given me to preach and teach on this vital subject around the world. It has become painfully apparent that even the best need encouragement—because life is tough and arduous at the best of times. Jesus Christ has something to say, and the life He promises gives us a hope and a future.

There are many people who have stood beside me and encouraged me as I have journeyed through life up to this point. They have been a constant reminder to me that God is faithful in every circumstance of life. My wife, Karyn, is my chief encourager, and I love her more today than when I first fell in love with her thirty-seven years ago!

My beloved congregation is a constant source of encouragement to me because of their mantra that "in Christ more is possible than you can ever imagine." It is hard to imagine such a large group of people, living with a determined oneness and unity in Christ, bound together by the conviction that God's Word is the only absolute truth upon which we stand. The ministry team includes my close friends and coworkers together in our combined effort to carry out the

Great Commission. I love them so much, even after all these years of serving the Lord Jesus together. I am very thankful, in particular, to Sam Davis, who is tireless in his capacity to assist me, and to Sharon Brisken, who continues to serve as my secretary with an uncommon faithfulness.

I continue to be so blessed by the life and ministry of Dr. Billy Graham. How profoundly grateful I am to be able to spend hours with him at his home in Montreat. His counsel to me about life and ministry constantly uplifts my soul-spirit and I love him deeply in my heart.

How can I ever thank the men and women who took time to write a note of personal endorsement for me or for this book? I realize fully the nature of busy schedules and commitments and want them to know that I appreciate their investment in getting the word out that we can over-come discouragement when we take God at His Word!

The entire staff at B&H is terrific! They have taken a preacher's heart and translated it into a reader's encourage-ment. I cannot thank Tom Walters, Kim Stanford, and the team enough for all the due diligence and patience. Their partnership with me has been a pleasure and I pray many people will be encouraged and strengthened in their walk with the Lord as a result.

Finally I thank my Lord and Savior for doing for me what I cannot do for myself. He has given me a hope and a future. I want you to know that what Jesus has done for me, He will do for you!

Contents

$\sim$

Setting the Scene

Do you ever get discouraged? Of course you do. The bullets fired out of the guns of life are many. You may be wounded and feel like you have been left to bleed alone, or you may simply be tired of dodging bullets. Is there hope for overcoming the discouragement you are feeling? The answer is yes, a thousand times yes!

Some have described life as either the rat race or the rut race. The former presents a picture of a desperate, round-the-clock effort to climb to the top of whatever the top may be. Many of the things we do in today's society epitomize the rat race! Observe the frenzy on any given day in a shopping mall. People hardly look at one another as they dash from one place to another in search of the right fit, something better, or the next best thing.

Too many people are desperately trying to climb the ladder of success without enough regard for their children who need *time* more than money, their wives who need a soft embrace more than sex in the city, or their husbands who need a castle to come home to more than a social climber to cling to.

The rut race is no different. You are stuck in a rut, and you know it. Every day seems no different from every other day. The second verse is just the same as the first verse. If it doesn't change, you are going to scream or do something crazy. The constant routine of getting up and going to the office or washing the clothes and straightening up the house is about to drive you up the wall. There has to be more to life.

You may drift into the soap-opera world and dream of the ideal husband, children, and job. You dream of that knight in shining armor riding up on his white horse, pulling you out of the rut, and carrying you off into the sunset. Then reality sets in, and you realize you are still in the rut, and nothing is going to change.

You may feel like Joseph when his brothers threw him into the pit, like life is over, and life as you know it will never be the same. Maybe you have lost your job, or a child has gone astray, or your spouse has told you that he or she is in love with someone else. You may have received the devastating news that you have a terminal illness, and you know you are facing terrible pain and hopelessness in the future.

Your rut can be a result of your own actions, or you may be completely innocent, a victim of someone else's sin. On the other hand, there may be no one to blame, and you begin to shoot the daggers of blame toward God. You wonder where to find that full and meaningful life described in the Bible.

There is a great plague of discouragement today, and if it has not engulfed you already, it most likely will at some time in your life. No one wants to be overwhelmed by this plague. But it's there.

A prison is a sad place in which to witness discouragement due to every malady known to mankind. There you will find a nation of people, just like you and me but with handcuffs on their wrists and ankles. The truth is, you actually don't have to be in a prison to be in the prison of discouragement. Whether you are on the inside of a prison or on the outside, handcuffs of the heart are the killers.

At least twice a year for many years, I have had the privilege of visiting and ministering in prisons across the United States of America. In the spring I travel to prisons with a wonderful group of senior adults called Yesterday's Teens. During the summer I accompany Mirror Image, a marvelous group of teens, as they do the same thing, mostly in Juvenile Detention Centers.

When the residents of these institutions march into the various facilities to visit and listen to us, you can sense the depression without even looking at their forlorn faces. It's pitiful to watch them. They are usually dressed in prison garb comprised of different color schemes suited to their sentences and the nature of their crimes. The prison guards hover about every entrance and exit. The chaplains are either incredible, God-fearing men or women who have a passion to minister to each individual, or their demeanor and attitude confirms the awful truth that they simply have a job.

From Starke and Miami Dade in Florida, to Cook County in Chicago, to Rikers Island in New York, to Tucker and Wrightsville in Arkansas, the soul searching is the same. Lines upon lines of men and women, boys and girls serving time for crimes against society. They file in and sit down like the young and the restless. Some are openly angry; some are just pleasantly docile. Some have smirks on their faces; some have numb expressions. Some nod their heads in welcoming hospitality, and some look daggers at you in a way that leaves you wondering if you will ever make it out of there alive.

As our presentation begins, some sing along with a loud voice while others stare in silence. Some tap their shoes in rhythm to the beat while others close their eyes as though bent on shutting out the sounds of hope and a future. Some are just as mad as, well, you know what! They are angry with the world, angry with the prison administration, angry with the judge who sent them there, angry with their lives or the lack thereof, and angry with themselves. Some are just sad. Mothers are separated from their little babies and children. Wives are separated from husbands. Daddies cannot care for their families. Teens are separated from their mothers and fathers. They are discouraged and weep because they have no hope.

When we visit prisons, our message is always the same whether we are in an adult male prison, women's prison, or a juvenile detention center. It always focuses on the cross of the Lord Jesus Christ. The message communicated in these prisons centers on the reality of their lives. These people, by and large, would not be the slightest bit impressed with church talk. I can't even imagine the looks on their faces if I stood to my feet and said, "Now let's turn in our Bibles to the third chapter of the book of John. And perhaps let's begin today's sermon with a little background on the life and times in which the apostle John penned these wonderful words, under the inspiration of the Spirit of the living God, who breathed the absolute inerrant and infallible word into the heart of His trusted servant."

They wouldn't understand.

This may be your problem too. You are listening to too much church talk, too much hype and not enough reality. And, perhaps, what we ministers need to do is realize there are some real hurting people out there who do not need another sermon or lecture but, rather, a fresh word of hope and encouragement from God.

That's what I want you to hear as you read this book. I want you to hear a fresh word from God, a fresh word of hope and encouragement.

I was born in Africa. Despite being surrounded by many opportunities, I just never seemed to fill the aloneness, the void in my life. I was a drifter. Like a nomad wandering in a vast desert, I wanted desperately to find an oasis to water my thirsty spirit. There had to be more to life. There had to be a greater purpose. My school days were a struggle, my military experience in the South African Army was too painful to believe it was actually happening to me, and my loving home had become little more than a boardinghouse.

But one day I ran headlong into the Lord Jesus Christ, and He changed my life forever. The emptiness ended. The longing was nullified. The pain of existence was removed. The agony of the search ended, and the cry of my heart was stilled. Jesus Christ came into my life, and everything changed. This is where a hope and a future begin.

What really intrigues me is how alike (outside and inside prisons) people in different parts of the world really are. As a boy I had no idea the extent to which the Lord would allow me to see this world in which we live. It's really amazing! People certainly look different. Many speak different languages, and it's hard to imagine eating some of the "delicacies" some people consider delicious.

The truth is, all people are looking for the same things.

Everywhere I have traveled I have found myself looking into the faces of people just like me. I find the same desperation, the same longing, the same emptiness, the same search, the same pain, the same anger, the same loneliness I had. It's the same stuff no matter where you have come from or where you think you are going. Life without Christ is like a vacuum cleaner without the electrical cord plugged in. It has no power to suck up the dirt. I believe all people are looking for answers to the same questions.

1. Is there such a thing as real love? Yes, there is! I have found it and believe that God will do the same thing for you that He has done for me. I have heard a number of incarcerated individuals bemoan the fact that the only love they ever encountered was a four-letter word! Many report a total absence of a father in their homes. One young man even told me he had never met his daddy and did not even know if he had one. Now that's something! Gangs form as a result of a lack of love and are a desperate measure for desperate hearts. Our hearts long for real love. God's love is the real thing. It is pure and holy; it is all that anyone could ever hope for.

So many people are discouraged because they have been deprived of love. As hard as it may seem to some, thousands of children have never heard their fathers say, "I love you!" How sad! God's love finds its root in His very existence. His love is who He is by nature. His essence is love, and all His attributes gush forth from the heart of His character, which is love.

2. Is there such a thing as real hope? Yes, there is! This is why I want you to read this book with an open heart.

Many years ago we were in a juvenile prison in Florida. As one can imagine, it takes a long time to get some one hundred visiting students through the security system. On this particular occasion the students had completed their security check, and I was the last person to go through into the prison. At the last moment a police vehicle suddenly drew up to the sidewalk and unloaded a young man.

Flanked by two burly police officers, this youth was chained up from head to toe. Not only did he have the usual handcuffs on his wrists, but there was a chain that looped from the handcuffs to his waist where chains literally wrapped around him a number of times. As if this was not enough to restrain this slightly built young man, another chain dangled down his legs and connected with some kind of ankle cuffs I had never seen before. He approached where I was standing with his head down and shuffled his feet as he moved past me in what can only be described as a doomsday silence.

After he passed, I asked one of the officers, "Who is that boy?"

"You don't want to know, Reverend," he replied.

"In fact, I do," I said politely, "I want to know who that boy is. I care about him."

"Well, that boy is no boy. He's seventeen years old. The first day he came into this place, he was just seven years old! Not long after he came in, we let him go home. But soon he was back in here again. You see, Reverend, these kids have no hope. They have nothing to go home to. This kid was in and out like a yo-yo. When he turned about thirteen, we let him go home again. Only this time he committed a violent crime. I was at his court appearance when the judge told him, 'Boy, you're a menace to society. I am tired of seeing your face, and so is the public. I am going to give you a life sentence. In fact, I am going to lock you up for so long you will forget who your mama is!'"

I was intrigued by this story. I had seen many young kids in prisons across America, but this one brought the reality of their plight home to me like never before.

"What's he doing here today?" I asked the officer.

"Well, Reverend," he continued, "this kid stayed in here until he was about seventeen. We were just about to send him up to the big boys at the state pen when the judge suddenly decided, through an appeal from some attorney, to let the boy go home. The judge thought the kid had learned his lesson and could be spared the trip up the road. "

"So when did he go home, Officer?"

"Yesterday, Reverend. He had no home to go to. He has no kinfolks."

He looked around and realized he was all alone in this world again. At least he had some buddies in prison and three square meals a day. So he walked across the road where an elderly woman was standing under a bus shelter. He just beat her up right there and waited for someone to call the cops. I got the call. When I arrived, he just stood there and looked at me. He made no effort to resist arrest and just held out his hands for me to cuff him.

"So that's it, Reverend. Pretty sorry, huh? This place is full of kids like this. No hope, no future!"

This officer came to hear Mirror Image present real hope and a real future to the inmates. Later that day he raised his hand when I asked if there were any who would like to give their hearts and lives to the Lord Jesus Christ, the only one who could offer real hope and a living future.

3. Is there such a thing as real forgiveness? Yes, there is! God's Son, the Lord Jesus Christ, laid down His life for you and me so that we can be completely forgiven of our sins. One thing is for sure. People have become geniuses in this world. Just think of all the brilliant discoveries and inventions that take place in our world. Man is capable of doing many wonderful things. He can send spaceships to the moon, he can find the cure for dreaded diseases, he can solve all kinds of mathematical problems, and he can travel anywhere he chooses. But there is one thing no person can do for himself or herself. You and I cannot forgive our own sin. We certainly try hard enough. Some people believe you can get forgiveness of sin by doing good deeds and works. Some wonderful people have denied themselves and have led exemplary lives of celibacy and restraint. Some have devoted themselves to missions in faraway places and become martyrs for causes far and wide. But no person can forgive himself or herself. There is not enough money you can give your church or favorite charity. It does not matter how many times you go to church. Forgiveness of sin cannot be granted by any person on this earth and cannot be earned by any action or activity, no matter how admirable it may be. Only Jesus Christ has God's full and complete authority to forgive sin. And this forgiveness is offered to all people who are willing to repent and turn to the Lord Jesus. This is what the Bible has to say about this reality: "Repent therefore and be converted, that your sins may be blotted out!" (Acts 3:19 NKJV).

When you are forgiven, Jesus Christ takes your sins, and He throws them all away forever. This may be hard to understand, but it is true. What an incredible hope and what a bright future!

4. *Is there such a thing as real respect?* Yes, there is! I encounter many people who suffer from disrespect. Thousands of men, women, and children are abused in ways we cannot even begin to imagine. Some disrespect is subtle and some painfully obvious. Many women, in particular, face disrespect from men who treat their wives and girlfriends as objects to be played with, used, and abused. The majority of women in prison yell out from the depths of their souls when I talk about this subject. Many years ago I was given a great lesson about respect.

In 1992 my family and I took a trip back to South Africa. En route, my oldest son, Rob, came to me and said, "Dad, President Nelson Mandela wants to talk to you!"

"Yea, right," I responded, "and my name is Muhammad Ali!" Well, as it turned out the about-to-be new president of South Africa did want to talk to me. He was just about the most famous person in the world at the time. Everybody had been rooting for him, and millions of people had watched his release from Robbin Island, a small prison fortress just off the coast of Cape Town.

Nelson Mandela and I had a great conversation. He is one impressive man! We talked about all kinds of things, but what impressed me most of all was his unbelievably humble spirit. I have told hundreds of inmates around the country that this was one black man who had every right to hate others. He and his friends had been chained up in prison for twenty-seven years. The prison they were in had no air conditioners. They had no amenities like the American prisons have today and were treated like animals most of the time. His release marked the beginning of a new day for South Africa. It was a new beginning in which reconciliation became the order of the day. The Truth and Reconciliation Commission, chaired by Archbishop Desmond Tutu, would conduct open inquiries into the atrocities of the apartheid system, and many people would come forward and be "forgiven" and reconciled.

But on this day Nelson Mandela had my attention. Among other things he mentioned the issue of respect. He told me that he believed people in the world needed to respect one another and that he would devote much of the rest of his life to this end. One of the things I heard he did shortly after his election as president was to call Mrs. Hendrik Verwoerd. This lady was the widow of the former prime minister of South Africa, Dr. Hendrik Verwoerd. This austere man was widely considered the architect of the apartheid system. So here was this black man, widely hated by the white establishment, imprisoned for twenty-seven years, and now with enough power to unleash massive retribution upon those who had locked him up. But he did not! He called Mrs. Verwoerd and asked her to come to Pretoria to have a meeting with him along with several other prominent people. When she declined, Mandela went to her home and had tea with her!

This story really touches me because I do not know whether or not Nelson Mandela is a Christian. If he is a Christian, I have never heard him testify to his faith in Christ Jesus. But his behavior certainly reflects the life of Christ when it comes to humility and respect and reconciliation.

This is one thing the Lord Jesus does for us. He levels the playing field when it comes to race, gender, and culture. There are so many divisions in this world and so many people spend half their lives hating one another and warring against one another. Just think of places like Ireland or India. Just look at your own neighborhood! When Jesus came into my heart and life, He did something for me in this department. He changed my attitude and gave me a new perspective of all people. I am still not perfect by any means and still struggle as all people do with built-in prejudices and biases. But the Lord has done something for me I would not be able to do for myself.

Yes, there is such a thing as respect!

5. Is there such a thing as a hope and a future? Yes, there is! All of the above affirm and confirm this fact. God is exactly who He says He is, and He offers all of us His hope and His future.

Part 1

Establishing Biblical Principles

Chapter One

Open Your Eyes

On the surface many struggle when it comes to being aware of and seeing their surroundings in a meaningful way. I live in the beautiful upstate region of South Carolina and am surrounded by mountains, rivers, lakes, and all of God's magnificent creation. As the years go by, I find myself taking many of these wonderful things for granted and the blessings of life becoming obscured. The business of life seems to chip away at my spirit. When the lights begin to dim, the fog sets in, and before too long everything becomes dreary and drab. It is time for our eyes to be opened.

Although any reference to a person's eyes carries the obvious idea of two organs attached to our faces, the Bible teaches the importance of the eyes of our hearts. One of my favorite hymns speaks of God opening the eyes of our hearts so that we can see Him. If we are really serious about finding a solution to the things that are weighing us down, we will need to pay special attention to this principle. We must ask the Lord to open the eyes of our hearts so that we may see not only our blessings that are on the surface but also those that are below the surface.

We must ask the Lord to help us see and interpret our lives through spiritual eyes. Paul had this in mind when he exhorted the Christians in Colossae:

> For this reason also, . . . we haven't stopped praying for you. We are asking that you may be filled with the knowledge of His will in all wisdom and spiritual understanding, so that you may walk worthy of the Lord, fully pleasing to Him, bearing fruit in every good work and growing in the knowledge of God. (Col. 1:9–10)

The ability to "walk" in a worthy manner can only be attained by opening your spiritual eyes. Only God can do this for you. He will do this for you if you ask Him. Having your spiritual eyes opened so that you can walk or live in a worthy manner produces fruitful work and an increased knowledge of God. This then produces fruit essential for every Christian's hope and future. These fruits, or by-products, are outworkings that express themselves in highly practical ways.

The first fruit has to do with the Scriptures. When God opens your spiritual eyes, you will develop a deeper love for the Word of God. The psalmist said it best:

> How I love Your teaching!
> It is my meditation all day long.
> Your command makes me wiser than my
>   enemies,
> for it is always with me.
> I have more insight than all my teachers
> because Your decrees are my meditation.
> I understand more than the elders
> because I obey Your precepts.
> I have kept my feet from every evil path
> to follow Your word.
> I have not turned from Your judgments,
> For You Yourself have instructed me.
> How sweet Your word is to me taste—
> sweeter than honey to my mouth.
> I gain understanding from Your precepts;
> therefore I hate every false way.
> Your Word is a lamp for my feet
> and a light on my path.
> (Ps. 119:97–105)

The second fruit relates to the challenging issue of obedience. This is such a key element of Christian discipleship. Disobedience to God's commands will diminish hope and a future because disobedience is sin in the eyes of the Lord. The more you fail to comply with the will of God, the more you will suffer the consequences. I am convinced disobedience is the main cause of deep distress and unhappiness.

David certainly attributed his loss of joy to his sin and disobedience. He begged the Lord to restore his joy following his sin of adultery. The apostle John took the matter even further when he correctly connected the question of obedience and salvation in the first of his three letters.

> This is how we are sure that we have come to
> know Him: by keeping His commands. The
> one who says, "I have come to know Him,"
> without keeping His commands, is a liar, and
> the truth is not in him. But whoever keeps His
> word, truly in him the love of God is perfected.
> This is how we know we are in Him: the one
> who says he remains in Him should walk just as
> He walked. (1 John 2:3–6)

The third fruit of spiritual growth is a strong understanding of the essential doctrines of the Bible. It has been said that "a weak theology will invariably lead to a weak lifestyle." This is so true! How many people have we heard of over the years who have fallen into the trap of shallow doctrine? Why would anyone want to behave accordingly if, in fact, they have nothing firm to stand on? A strong foundation provides security. How can anyone have any real hope without a strong foundation? Once again John continues this theme.

> I am writing to you, little children, because
> your sins have been forgiven on account
> of His name. I am writing to you, fathers,
> because you have come to know the One who
> is from the beginning. I am writing to you,
> young men, because you have had victory over
> the evil one. I have written to you, children,
> because you have come to know the Father.
> I have written to you, fathers, because you
> have come to know the One who is from the
> beginning. I have written to you, young men,
> because you are strong, God's Word remains
> in you, and you have had victory over the evil
> one. (1 John 2:12–14)

The fourth fruit concerns the growth of one's faith. When Jesus Christ enters the heart of an individual, that person is "born again" and becomes as a newborn baby. In a spiritual sense that person's life has only just begun. Growth must take place in order for that person to become complete. Sadly, many Christians remain spiritual infants even though they occupy adult bodies. Such people seldom have any real hope in the things that matter most. Perhaps this will explain why so many of them spend so much of their time squawking and complaining their way through life, especially in the church! In his commendation of the new believers in Thessalonica, Paul raved, "We must always thank God for you, . . . which is fitting, since your faith is flourishing, and the love of every one of you for one another is increasing" (2 Thess. 1:3). In his letter to the Corinthian Christians, Paul addressed the problem of people in the church who had not grown in their faith:

> Now I, Paul, make a personal appeal to you
> by the gentleness and graciousness of Christ—
> I who am humble among you in person, but
> bold toward you when I am absent. I beg you
> that when I am present I will not need to be
> bold with the confidence by which I plan to
> challenge certain people who think we are
> walking in a fleshly way. For although we are
> walking in the flesh, we do not wage war in a
> fleshly way, since the weapons of our warfare
> are not fleshly, but are powerful through God
> for the demolition of strongholds. We demolish
> arguments and every high-minded thing that is
> raised up against the knowledge of God, taking
> every thought captive to the obedience of
> Christ. (2 Cor. 10:1–5)

The final fruit is the growing love Christians have for one another. To the people of Philippi Paul wrote, "And I pray this: that your love will keep on growing in knowledge and every kind of discernment, so that you can determine what really matters and can be pure and blameless in the day of Christ, filled with the fruit of righteousness that comes through Jesus Christ, to the glory and praise of God" (Phil. 1:9–11).

Ask God to open your eyes so that you can take a hard look at yourself and so that you can take a hard look at Him. Whatever your circumstances, God is there with the strength to carry you through. You can depend on Him. He is standing willing and able to bring you through whatever circumstances you are facing.

Chapter Two

Talk to God

Having established the critical importance of opening your eyes to the reality of your circumstances, our attention now turns to another biblical principle of immense importance. We discussed in the last chapter the importance of focusing on God and depending on His power to make it through the struggles of life, but there is another step to acquiring the power from God needed to make it through life with hope and a future—talking to God. Talking to God, prayer, unlocks the key to God's heart.

Some might be of the opinion that the subject of prayer is beyond them or, perhaps, ought to be reserved for a select few who really need to hear more about it. Not so fast! Prayer continues to be the greatest struggle of my own life, and I believe it continues to be the missing element in the lives of most believers and their churches. I will readily admit that I have no excuse despite the fact that I find myself lining up one excuse after another as to why I do not spend more time in my prayer closet. Prayer is the prime means by which we are able to talk to our heavenly Father, and it remains the prime means by which we are able to hear from our heavenly Father. My number one excuse is busyness. It's that old schedule thing. Doing this and doing that for the Lord. After all, the Lord knows I am serving Him, doesn't He?

It is hard to believe that a man like Nehemiah in the Bible found the time to pray at all. He was under siege! He was being bombarded by bombshells from every conceivable side of his life. The goons were after him in a big way and had made it their business to hammer down on him. Nothing was going to hinder their attack, and their goal remained solid. Take the man down!

So here we find Nehemiah faced with sarcasm, anger, hostility, ridicule, and downright rank ugliness doing what he had to do without question. It may be helpful to note some of the vital elements of the prayer he prayed.

Vital Elements of Nehemiah's Prayer

"Listen, our God, for we are despised. Make their insults return on their own heads and let them be taken as plunder to a land of captivity" (Neh. 4:4).

1. A Prayer to Be Heard

Hear the passion expressed as Nehemiah begins his prayer with, "Listen, our God." What the man says and how he says it are important to us as we think about our own lives and situations. A closer reading of the text leaves one with the distinct impression that Nehemiah might have forgotten himself for just a minute. Maybe he almost sounds a little angry or demanding of God. But let's not forget how desperate the man was. And don't you think God would have known how desperate he was? I think so. God always understands what we are going through. Jesus came to this earth and identified with us in all our human struggles without ever laying aside His sinlessness. He knows our condition, and He knows our hearts. Don't hold back. As long as your expression is an expression of personal agitation and hurt and not an expression of hostility and sin toward God, have at it! Tell the Lord what is in your heart.

2. A Prayer of Admission

What follows from the heart of Nehemiah is important. "For we are despised," the man admitted to God. There was no holding back from the bottom line of his predicament. "This is what is happening to us," he confessed to the Lord, as if God did not already know all about it. This is the thing about reaching the point of admission. God already knows about it all. So why in the world would you not tell Him about it all? Children so often fall into this trap with their mothers, especially. One can just picture this little boy with his face covered in chocolate when his mother walks in and says, "Son, did you happen to see what happened to the chocolate I left on the table?" "No, Mama," he replies, with a look of puzzlement as to why his mother has a grin on her face. So "fess up" to the Lord and begin with an outright admission of exactly what is going on in your life.

3. A Prayer of Frustration

Discouragement leaves us frustrated, sometimes in a serious way. The thing about pain and hurt that will not go away is that it produces an inner weariness. When the days turn into months and the months turn into years and the years turn into decades, the rub turns to heat, and the heat hurts. I have met some dear people who have suffered for years on end. They have sought out every kind of help imaginable with little positive result. This wears the soul down and grinds the heart into pulp. Frustration is a real thing even in the lives of the strongest believers. You can hear this frustration when you read this prayer offered by Nehemiah. Don't be afraid to vent your frustration to God. He understands you and loves you with all your frustrations.

4. A Prayer of Direction

This is an interesting element of Nehemiah's prayer of anguish. Read it closely, and you cannot help but hear the manner with which he appears to tell God what God needs to do. It sounds awfully cheeky, if you ask me. I mean who does the man really think he is, regardless of his situation? Any normal person would not just turn to God and start telling him what to do! But he did just exactly that! "Make their insults return on their own heads." "Let them be taken as plunder to a land of captivity" (4:4). "Do not cover their guilt or let their sin be erased from Your sight" (4:5). Ouch!

Let me attempt a rough translation. In modern-day terminology this element might have sounded something like this: "OK God, I have been deeply hurt and offended by these idiots, but this is not just about me. My whole family has been affected. Here I am, serving You and being obedient to the point of no return, and these characters are hounding me, insulting me, and making my life an utter misery. This is frustrating me beyond reason. I am getting more depressed by the minute, and, quite frankly, I do not know how much more I can take. Zap them for me and get them real good. Have absolutely no mercy on them whatsoever!"

Phew! This may shock some people, but how else can this aspect of his prayer be depicted? The point, once again, revolves around the reality of his pain. This man was not caught up in some childish prank with Sanballat and his brood of vipers. Neither is your pain. It is real, and perhaps one of the hardest things you have to deal with are people who just don't seem to understand what you are going through. Don't depend on them. Thank the Lord for family and friends who "know what lies beneath," but don't depend on them. People will always let you down. Depression and discouragement can be awfully lonely experiences. God knows and understands even when you lecture Him on solutions you think most appropriate.

5. A Prayer of Deliverance

Nehemiah's prayer comes full circle in that it is ultimately a prayer for deliverance. It is essentially a desperate cry for help. In my mind I see the man prostrate before God, perhaps with his face on the ground and in the mud as he cries out for God to "hear us"! Remember that God is the one who looks all the way into the heart. He made us and constructed even the minutest details of our being. The hand of the one who made the heavens and the earth handcrafted us. As John reported in his prologue, "Through him all things were made; without him nothing was made that has been made" (John 1:3 NIV). Whatever Nehemiah may have said in his hour of desperation and whatever we may think about it, his prayer screams with a plea for deliverance.

When you find yourself without much hope and sadly lacking in any concept of a bright and happy future, get down before the Lord and plead with Him to deliver you. He wants to and He will! Nehemiah did and so can you!

My favorite reminder of the meaning of prayer came out of the mouth of my daughter Shelley when she was just a small child. I remember the occasion well. It was one of those special days when little girls are given special permission by mom to go and spend the night with a friend. I think they called these events "sleepovers." Off she toddled with great excitement and untold joy at the prospect of having so much fun with her little girlfriends. When she arrived back home the next day, she immediately came bounding up to me as only Daddy's little girl can do and said, "Daddy, Daddy, please can I get a kitty?"

"A kitty?" I inquired.

"Yes, Daddy, a cute, little kitty—just like Susie's kitty."

I confess that my response was anything but gracious or loving. In the first instance, I was not all that well disposed to cats. In the second instance, we already had a fine puppy by the name of Bully.

"And besides, Shelley, within a day or two you will have lost interest in the kitty, and then guess who is going to be left holding the kitty?" I broke my little princess's heart!

God has a great sense of humor. A few weeks later, I came home from the office and was walking through the garage into the house from the back door. As I passed by one of the piles of "stuff" which typifies many a garage, I was struck by the strangest sound. *Hello there,* I thought, *what in the world is that sound?* It sounded like something being scraped and scratched. The scratching sound was coming from a box at the bottom of a pile of other boxes. I pulled the box out and discovered something to my absolute amazement.

You've got it!

A stray mother cat had found herself an ideal place to give birth—not to one or two kitties, not to three or four kitties. No indeed! But to five of the tiniest, cutest kitties one could ever imagine!

Well! What could this daddy do but make the announcement to Shelley. I wish I could describe the picture of utter joy and abandoned ecstasy. She took one look at them and ran around and around the garage floor clapping her hands while doing a little dance. She was so happy! And, I might add, she included a sweet little three-word chorus of thanksgiving as part of her repertoire, "Thank you, Daddy! Thank you, Daddy!"

That afternoon Karyn and I loaded up Shelley to go to the airport to meet our new children's minister, Keith. Keith just loved little kids, and they took to him like bees to honey. Karyn and I sat in the front seat while Keith and Shelley took up their place on the backseat. As we drove off, Shelley turned to Keith and said something like this.

"Guess what, Mr. Keith?"

"What, Shelley?"

"Well, I've always wanted a kitty. And so I prayed and prayed and prayed, and guess what, Mr. Keith? God gave me five kitties!"

And with that I turned to my wife and said, "I hope she's not praying for a little brother!"

Isn't it amazing to listen to the raw honesty of a child?

In my book *When God Prayed,* I wrote about many aspects of prayer as they flowed from the heart of the Lord Jesus just prior to His betrayal. The issue that stood out for me most of all is the fact that our Savior is, Himself, interceding for us. The Lord Jesus went obediently to the cross to complete His work for the redemption of man. When He made that wonderful pronouncement, "It is finished," the Lord Jesus was announcing the complete success of His work and mission in the accomplishment the Father had required of Him. Sinful man now had access to the Father through the shed blood of the Lord Jesus Christ. But His ministry of intercession would continue, as it does today, as the Son speaks to the Father on behalf of all those He loves.

Talking to God is critical when it comes to everything, especially in regards to our hope and future. When you find you are losing hope and becoming down and depressed, talk to God. He loves you. He is listening to you. He wants to help you.

Chapter Three

Never Lose Heart

S o we rebuilt the wall until the entire wall was joined together up to half its height, for the people had the will to keep working" (Neh. 4:6).

Nehemiah and his people kept on keeping on! "For the people had the will to keep on working." Wow!

The will to keep on working must have been tough. They were being hammered and harassed. Sanballat, Tobiah, and the entire mob of their henchmen were pounding away at this group of God's servants. And yet they kept on going. What a testimony! They were mocked, belittled, and even threatened, but they never gave up!

Perhaps this sounds just like you and your circumstances. The attacks of Satan can be relentless, and the one thing he would want you to do is give up! I have experienced this in my own life. There have been times when my studies have simply become too much. There have been times when my ministry has weighed me down to the point at which I wanted to quit.

Many years prior to Nehemiah, we find Moses experiencing the same challenges. He had grown up in the lap of luxury in Pharaoh's court but came to the point at which he realized God had a plan and purpose for his life. He knew God had spoken to him, and he knew God had called him to a life of service. He realized he could not stay where he was in Egypt and serve God at the same time. He understood, I think, that things could never be the same again and that he would have to forfeit all the power and privilege afforded him. But he had seen the great "I am" and "considered reproach for the sake of the Messiah to be greater wealth than the treasures of Egypt, since his attention was on the reward" (Heb. 11:26). So Moses' choice was not even a choice. He left Egypt and accepted God's commission to lead the children of Israel from bondage to freedom. And then, even after he turned his back on his power and privilege, he still pursued God's call and will with a relentless determination. He was confronted many times by the naysayers. The Israelites mumbled, grumbled, and groaned their way across the desert. They fought with one another, fussed about everything imaginable, doubted God from one sand dune to another, and attacked Moses' credibility without shame or remorse. And yet God's servant kept on keeping on.

The supreme example of perseverance is the Lord Jesus Christ who went to the cross despite the pain and humiliation He suffered at the hands of men. The Thessalonian Christians were pounded relentlessly as well. They suffered persecution and humiliation for their faith. They were bombarded by false prophets who tried to convince them that the judgment of the Lord had already taken place and some of them even tried to fake the hand of Paul's writing, but they kept on keeping on. This is one of the reasons Paul was able to say to them, "We have confidence in the Lord about you, that you are doing and will do what we command. May the Lord direct your hearts to God's love and Christ's endurance" (2 Thess. 3:4–5).

If you want to think about never losing heart, just think about Eli Manning. You may not be a football fan, but few people will ever forget the Super Bowl where the New York Giants prevailed against the highly favored New England Patriots. Most fans had grown accustomed to seeing the previous year's Most Valuable Player, Peyton Manning, throw one touchdown after another as his Colts went on to win the coveted prize. Eli seemed destined to live in his older brother's shadow and ride the coattails of his famous father, the former New Orleans Saint, Archie Manning. The game went down to the last minute. Both teams had played well. But it took a "never quit" attitude on the part of one determined quarterback. The play that won the day will go down in history. How Manning was not sacked is amazing, but he broke all tackles and hoisted the ball into the hands of his receiver who held on in an amazing way! Eli Manning was the new Most Valuable Player of the National Football League, all because he never gave up.

Chapter Four

Remember Who God Is

One of the most important things to do when hope fails is to remember who God is. The story of Nehemiah's determination is remarkable. The relentless onslaught of his enemies must have brought him to the point of despair. Even after they had rebuilt the wall and had determined to keep on keeping on, Sanballat and his bunch "became furious." The word here has little kindness attached to it. These men were mean to the core. They had no sympathy for the workers whatsoever and made it their business to destroy them if at all possible. The Scriptures tell us that "they all plotted together to come and fight against Jerusalem and throw it into confusion" (Neh. 4:8).

Nehemiah's enemies said, "They won't know or see anything until we're among them and can kill them and stop the work" (v. 11). Things became so bad that the Jews who lived nearby concluded that they could not turn in any direction without the imminent threat of being attacked and killed.

At this point of desperation and despair, God's servant stood to his feet and made the most incredible declaration:

> After I made an inspection, I stood up and said
> to the nobles, the officials, and the rest of the
> people, "Don't be afraid of them. Remember
> the great and awe-inspiring Lord, and fight for
> your countrymen, your sons and daughters,
> your wives and homes." (Neh. 4:14)

What leadership! I love the fact that this man stood up and faced the enemy head on. The perspective he gave to them focused squarely on our God, and the determination with which he said what he said must have left all of them in a state of awe! The reason they did not need to be afraid was that God is God, and He has not changed His mind! What a sermon in one sentence!

Look what happened as a result. "When our enemies realized that we knew their scheme and that God had frustrated it, every one of us returned to his own work on the wall" (v. 15). The enemy was totally thwarted by the Lord God. He who frustrated them in their evil schemes, and He empowered the people to return to their stations. It is amazing what God can do. All we need to do is remember who He is. One of the ploys of Satan is to cause doubt and distrust of God to rear its ugly head in our hearts.

The Israelites experienced this over and again as they wandered through the wilderness. Every time they won a battle or saw the mighty hand of God at work, that old devil would interfere and distract them. He would raise up Sanballats and Tobiahs to question God in every way. Satan has done this from the beginning when he accosted Eve in the garden of Eden. His tactic was to cause Eve to doubt God's authority. "Now the serpent was the most cunning of all the wild animals that the LORD God had made. He said to the woman, 'Did God really say, "You can't eat from any tree in the garden"?'" (Gen. 3:1).

I pray you will not be blindsided by the devil's tactics to cause you to doubt God's authority and power to give you a hope and a future. I pray God will open the eyes of your heart to see who He really is and what He wants to do in and through your life.

Chapter Five

Make Preparation

Throughout this story we find Nehemiah in a constant state of preparation, regardless of their progress. At the outset of his dealings with Sanballat and Tobiah, when things were just beginning to warm up, we read, "So we prayed to our God and stationed a guard because of them day and night" (Neh. 4:9). We have already emphasized the importance of prayer in terms of preparation, but Nehemiah took the matter one big step further. He stationed a guard to watch out for them around the clock. He was not prepared to let his guard down, not for a second. Perhaps he realized the tenacity of Satan. Perhaps he understood the vulnerability of his people. Perhaps he knew how weak they really were without the necessary fortifications. The point is, he was not willing to take a chance with the devil.

Herein lies one of the major reasons Paul was so insistent about putting on "the whole armor of God" (Eph. 6:11 KJV). We will talk about this in a later chapter because it is critical for every believer to understand that God has made available to us the best equipment to guard us against the onslaught of the evil one.

Later on we find Nehemiah almost at the point of taking extreme measures:

> So we continued the work, while half of the
> men were holding spears from daybreak until
> the stars came out. At that time, I also said to
> the people, "Let everyone and his servant spend
> the night inside Jerusalem, so that they can
> stand guard by night and work by day." And
> I, my brothers, my men, and the guards with
> me never took off our clothes. Each carried his
> weapon, even when washing. (Neh. 21–23)

How far are you and I willing to go when it comes to preparation? Nehemiah was not willing to relax at any time, day or night. So many of us find ourselves struggling, and yet we let our guard down. Sometimes this may happen for just a brief moment, but it provides enough of a keyhole for that old serpent to crawl though and make mischief. Here are a few suggestions on how we can make preparation every day.

1. Pray every day. Just share your heart with the Lord. Tell Him about your day. Share some of the decisions you have to make. Talk to Him as though you are talking to your best friend because He is your best friend. Don't get caught up in words. Just talk! Tell Him all about your struggles, and don't be concerned that your prayer is either too long or too short. Just pray! And do this when you get up in the morning.

2. Read God's Word every day. Open your Bible to any book in the Bible. I suggest Philippians or John in the New Testament or the Psalms or Nehemiah in the Old Testament. Actually it doesn't matter which part of the Bible you turn to because everything in God's Word will bless you. There are also many devotional books available. They have a Bible passage for you to read and then have a short comment on that Bible passage. *The Encouraging Word*, my television ministry, has a wonderful Bible devotional to offer you, and it's free just for the asking. Of course there are many others that I would recommend. The point is that a short reading every day will fortify you and will help you be properly prepared for the day. You will be amazed at the things the Lord will say to you each day through His Word.

3. Start a daily journal. Go to your favorite Christian bookstore and buy a small notebook. These are inexpensive, and, if you buy a small one, you will even be able to carry it with you in your pocket or purse as you travel about your daily routine. After you have talked to God and read a Bible passage, take a page of your notebook and write the date in the top corner. In this way you will accumulate a daily record. Then write down just a few of the thoughts you have in mind after you have read your Bible and prayed. It really doesn't matter how you do this. There are no rules about how you journal. The important thing is to write down your thoughts. Take special note of some of your concerns and struggles. Then write down some of the things you feel the Lord has said to you, either in your heart through prayer or by means of the passage you have just read. I have some friends who write their concerns and requests down on one side of the page, and then they write down the answer to those concerns or the solution, as needed. Keeping a journal is simple and can be accomplished in a variety of ways. Finding a way that suits your personal taste is the best way to go. The bottom line is the fact that you journal.

4. Choose a prayer partner. Select one other person to join you in your new effort to be better prepared for daily living. But I must insist that you choose this person carefully. He or she does not have to be a family member. Some have even recommended that this person not be your spouse, and I would tend to agree with this. There is no hard and fast rule here. In my case, my wife is my closest friend. But both she and I need to have an outside person to talk to and share with. Confidentiality is not an option. It is a mandate that must be agreed to and upheld, no matter what happens.

The benefits of being able to have someone walk alongside you are immeasurable and far-reaching. I suggest you meet with your prayer partner at least once a week. I have a friend who meets with his prayer partner every Tuesday morning for breakfast at a local restaurant. They carry their journals to breakfast, and each takes a turn to read out loud their last week's entries. They celebrate together, commiserate together, petition the Lord together, and weep together! My friend has never told me one single thing they have talked about or even discussed because they have made a covenant together to hold in sacred trust the things they talk about. He tells me he now has another journal exclusively for the things that his prayer partner needs for him to pray about on his prayer partner's behalf.

These are simple tasks, but they carry a profound return investment. God will bless you if you do these things. He will lift you up and out of the sea of despair you may find yourself in. He will encourage your heart if you are discouraged. He will renew your sense of hope and a future if you are having difficulty seeing beyond the veil of time. He will fortify you, even if you are enjoying a fruitful and blessed time in your life. He will give you strength for the journey. Never think you have ever arrived at the point at which you are adequately prepared. Stay prepared daily!

Chapter 6

Stick to the Assignment

D on't "chop and change" from one thing to another. I believe one of the most disheartening things to do in life is to keep on moving to some place else to do something else. Playing the game of golf is probably one of the joys of my life. I love just getting out there, especially with a group of friends, just to have fun. I do not like playing with people who think the world is about to come to an end just because they have not brought their "A" game along with them for the day. But I do love the sport. My biggest challenge in golf is the golden rule of golf: "Play the ball where it lies!" Now I must confess that I try to do my best in this department, but I have failed far too many times. My "foot wedge" has a habit of suddenly jumping into action, especially when needed!

Many people have a "foot wedge" approach to life. They are generally dissatisfied people who are constantly looking out for something bigger and better. Paul emphasized the importance of contentment when he wrote his letter from prison:

> I don't say this out of need, for I have learned
> to be content in whatever circumstances
> I am. I know both how to have a little, and
> I know how to have a lot. In any and all
> circumstances I have learned the secret of being
> content—whether well-fed or hungry, whether
> in abundance or in need. I am able to do all
> things through Him who strengthens me.
> (Phil. 4:11–13)

I believe the Lord gives to each one of His children a series of assignments during their journey of life. He never gives us more than we can handle at one time. Now, while I cannot suggest that the Lord gives us only one major thing to do at a time, I am certain He has our interest at heart. He would never, for example, ask us to do something that would destroy our families. But He certainly calls some to lead lives on the edge for His sake. Does He bring some assignments to a close and then open others? Of course He does. But whatever you are doing for Him, do it as though it will be the only thing God ever asks you to do. Unpack your bags for life until the Lord tells you otherwise! Stick to your assignment! Nehemiah could have jumped ship with great reason. Few would have questioned his right to privacy. Few would have argued as to the cruel nature of the onslaught against him. Few would have called him on the carpet and given him a lecture about the broken walls. Who really knows? He had every right to back off and back down and give up the struggle. But he did not! He stuck to the assignment.

Here are a few suggestions that may help you to stick to the assignment:

1. *Make sure you are doing what God told you to do.* Go back to the point at which you first arrived where you are. Get out a notebook and write down the events and circumstances that caused you to make the move to where you are. What attracted you there? Did God have any role in your decision? What was your primary motivation? Was it money, status, the place, or comfort? What was it exactly?

2. *Make a note of all your accomplishments and failures where you are.* Don't hold back and be perfectly honest about these things. It will not help you to hide anything from yourself. Are you able to establish a pattern of success or failure at this point? If you are able to chart a pattern of success, you are probably in the right place for the time being. If not, you are most assuredly in the wrong place.

3. *Make an effort to write down a vision for the future.* This will flow out of your heart if you are in the right place and you were able to establish a pattern of success. If you are unable to write down a fresh vision for the days that lie ahead, this may mean the Lord is telling you it is time to

move to another assignment. On the other hand, if a fresh vision flows out of your heart, it is most likely the Lord has you right where He wants you to be.

If you are sure you are doing what God has told you to do, stick to the assignment. Never give up!

Chapter Seven

Claim the Victory

This is the point I love! We serve a victorious God. The battle is won! Read Nehemiah's remarkable account:

> The laborers who carried the loads worked with one hand and held a weapon with the other. Each of the builders had his sword strapped around his waist while he was building, and the trumpeter was beside me. Then I said to the nobles, the officials, and the rest of the people: "The work is enormous and spread out, and we are separated far from one another along the wall. Wherever you hear the trumpet sound, rally to us there. Our God will fight for us!" (Neh. 4:17–20)

What a story of unbridled faith, trust, and hope. This man had put his trust in God and carried that trust right onto his battlefield. His belief in God's ability to do what only God can do caused him to place a trumpeter in a strategic position, not for a probability but for a certainty! Nehemiah had no doubt that his God would carry the day.

The believers in Rome during Paul's day were also faced with uncertainty and despair. They were being accosted and persecuted for their faith in every way. This is why Paul was able to share this wonderful news with them:

> No, in all these things we are more than
> victorious through Him who loved us. For
> I am persuaded that neither death nor life, nor
> angels nor rulers, nor things present, nor things
> to come, nor powers, nor height, nor depth,
> nor any other created thing will have the power
> to separate us from the love of God that is in
> Christ Jesus our Lord! (Rom. 8:37–39)

What calm assurance! Perhaps it is time for you to claim the victory in Christ. Perhaps it is time to rise up from your bed and stand in the presence of the One who gives you strength. Perhaps it is time to lay aside the things that have been holding you down all these years. Surrender them to the One who is victorious.

In summary, we have considered the biblical principles that will establish a foundation for hope and a future.

The question we now have to face concerns the practical application of these principles. In the next section we will apply the things we have learned to our everyday lives.

Part 2

Making Practical Applications

Introduction

We have looked at biblical truths about overcoming discouragement. These truths are essential for giving us a solid foundation. The pain, suffering, and discouragement so many endure demands that a biblical foundation must be built upon which to stand. I want to add here that there are many wonderful, fully qualified Christian counselors in our communities, and I want to affirm my personal appreciation for them. Many of these people are qualified to help us deal with the vast variety of needs we have, and, perhaps most important of all, I believe many are uniquely called of God to serve in the capacity of counselor. So go to them and listen to them and try to follow their advice if it lines up with biblical principles. This will serve you well. God has always used people to help other people, especially when faced with discouragement. But always remember, it is the Word of God that stands the test of time and is the counsel that never fails.

Now it is time to put some of the things we have learned so far into practice. This is, perhaps, one of the most difficult things to do for many people. It is one thing to read what God has to say to us, but it is a different story to go out and put these truths into practice.

What we have to do is take action!

This reminds me of Jesus' extraordinary preaching of the Sermon on the Mount. Jesus' message here is one of the most quoted in the entire world. The whole message is recorded in Matthew's Gospel from chapter 5 through chapter 7. A wide range of subject matter is covered, and its content includes just about everything needed for mankind to live according to the standards set by our God. But when Jesus gets toward the end of the sermon, He suddenly issues a direct challenge: "Enter through the narrow gate. For the gate is wide and the road is broad that leads to destruction, and there are many who go through it. How narrow is the gate and difficult is the road that leads to life, and few find it" (Matt. 7:13–14).

Here Jesus is demanding that a decision be made. Action is demanded. Jesus is talking about salvation. The choice is clear. You are either for God or against God. But Jesus' plea for action also highlights another important thing. Without suggesting that I could ever put words into Jesus' mouth, this is what I hear Him saying to all people in the Sermon on the Mount: "Ladies and gentlemen, it has been My honor and privilege to preach this message to you today. Thank you for being attentive, but your willingness to pay attention is not enough to get you into heaven. You must take action! I am also grateful for the respect you have afforded Me as a visiting preacher. But respect for Me is not good enough to get you into heaven. You must make a choice and take action! Many of you admire Me and appreciate the hard work and effort involved in the work I do, but this is not good enough to get you into heaven. You have to take action! As I have watched you, I see that many of you genuinely accept what I am saying. You believe that this is a Word from the Father in heaven, and you believe it is correct, good, and accurate. You have no argument with the ethics presented or the doctrine stated. This is good, but it is not good enough to get you into heaven. You have to make a choice. You must take action. You must enter through the narrow gate. This narrow gate is the only way made possible through My sacrifice that is to come through the shedding of My blood for you. I am the only way to heaven."

Sounds like the church in America today! We are willing to listen, but few take any real action.

And so it is when it comes to this issue of overcoming discouragement. If you genuinely desire to stand up even though you have fallen down, you must listen and then take action. Now it is time to put some of these things we've considered into action.

Chapter One

Check Your Own Spiritual Energy Level

For many years I have dreamed about purchasing a good motorcycle. I love the things! Perhaps it's that my dad as a young man raced motorbikes with great success. Regardless, I have always loved riding big, solid, thundering, "hog-eating" motorbikes. To me there is nothing quite like thundering down the Blue Ridge Parkway with the wind in my face. Sounds like a midlife crisis, doesn't it?

I remember when my wife and I were first married in Africa. Almost every week we would pack a backpack and head up into the mountains on our bike. On weekends we would hop on the bike and cruise through the

African bush down to the beautiful Indian Ocean. It was wonderful!

But I will always remember one bad moment when I was a senior in high school. I had a motorcycle in high school. It was the only way we could get around, other than a bicycle, and of course, that was out of the question for a senior! On one particularly hot summer day, I found myself about a mile from my home when all of a sudden my bike just spluttered and stopped. In my day we had to wear school uniforms replete with a black jacket, long-sleeved shirt, tie, and a pair of long, grey flannel trousers. And so in this out-fit I began to push my motorbike up the long road toward my home where I finally arrived. Talk about down in the dumps. I was depressed and angry. And so I began to dis-mantle my bike to find out what was wrong. Every piece had to come off, one by one. When most of the bike had been dismantled, I sunk to the ground in despair and just sat exhausted on the grass. As I sat there feeling sorry for myself, I felt a cool shadow move over me, and I looked up into the face of my dad.

"Having a problem, Son?"

"The stupid thing just quit on me, Dad!"

"Have you checked to see if there is any gas in the tank?"

Now, folks, I know some of you think this is funny. I want you to know I am still trying to get over this! But through it all and especially now in my later life, I get it. Oftentimes, when life brings discouragement, we manage to go on even though life is hard, but other times we sputter and stop. We try to figure out what is wrong to no avail. Let me make a suggestion. Could it possibly be that you have run out of gas? Spiritual gas! Your tank is empty. Before you take everything apart trying to decide what is wrong, check your spiritual gas tank! You can do something about it! I want to encourage you not to sit down in the grass and give up. Feel the cool shadow of your heavenly Father standing over you with the answer to your problem. Spiritual gas. Spiritual energy.

I am a blessed man in more ways than I could ever deserve, but even though I'm so incredibly blessed, my spiritual energy can run low, and I am susceptible to burning out. Born in Africa to wonderful parents, I grew up having a life filled with adventure of every kind. My dad was gloriously saved by the Lord despite having led a life almost totally void of any concern about the things of God up until that point. With Mom at his side, he gave his life to full-time Christian service and ministry so that my brothers and I grew up in a home where the Lord Jesus was practiced and proclaimed.

As a young boy, I went to boarding school in the magnificent hills of Zululand and then on to a prestigious high school for boys. By God's grace and despite so many battles as a teenager, I graduated. By God's grace alone I survived an awful experience as a soldier in the border regions of Angola and went on to a university where I fell in love with the most beautiful girl I had ever seen. When the Lord called

Karyn and me into the ministry, we could not have considered ourselves more honored. It seems that everywhere the Lord has allowed us to serve has turned out to be a blessing of unwarranted proportion. We have seen the hand of the Lord times without number and firmly believe it is all because of His grace alone.

Ministry is jolly hard work! It involves working for the King of kings and the Lord of lords and it involves people! Enough said! It is blessed but also hard work visiting, loving, listening, and working with people.

Is it possible to be empowered to love people, to serve them, to reach out and touch their lives, and then to burnout spiritually?

So, if I am not afraid of jolly hard work, and if I am willing to do whatever it takes to share the love of Christ with a lost and dying world, and if I am willing to roll up my sleeves and join together with thousands of wonderful people in the building of the church of God, then what seems to be the problem!

Spiritual burnout!

Did you know you and I could get so close to the Word of God that it ends up becoming fuzzy when we read it? Did you know that you could pray with other people so much and so often that your own prayer life suffers and takes a backseat? Did you know that you could literally spend hours listening to the problems of others so much that you actually don't recognize the problems in your own life? Did you know you could offer the absolute best advice and counsel to others while at the same time neglecting the counsel you need for your own life and well-being? Of course you do!

In my case I am deeply grateful that the symptoms of spiritual exhaustion or burnout were recognized and addressed. This is what spiritual exhaustion can do to you:

- It can take the smile off your face.
- It can seriously affect your relationships.
- It can cause you to lose your job.
- It can make you do foolish things.
- It can drive you to despair.
- It can make you question God.
- It can cause you to doubt your faith.
- It can change your disposition and character.

Here are some of the signs you need to be aware of:

1. You could begin to find it more and more difficult to go to sleep at night. When you do go to sleep you will often fall into a deep, almost unconscious sleep, to begin with. Then you will suddenly wake up as though someone had walked into your room and switched on the lights. What follows is even more difficult to cope with. Your mind will latch on to something. This "something" could be anything. Sometimes the thing you cannot get out of your head is as trivial as walking up a set of stairs or trying to tie a shoelace. Perhaps it could be a Bible study class you lead and teach or a mission class you are involved with or some act of service you offer. The problem here is not the fact that these things come to mind but that, once they do, your mind latches on to them and will not let go.

2. It follows that you could then become sleep deprived. When this happened to me, I found that I would toss and turn until the early hours of the morning, at which time I would fall into a sleep so deep that I struggled to wake up at the appropriate time. This began to increase to the point that I was becoming more and more exhausted and less and less helpful in the home.

3. The next major area that can become affected is your physical well-being. I am going to spend quite a bit of time on this later so I will just mention it at this point.

What you will find is that all of these symptoms begin to run together. Some are more serious than others, but they all have their role to play in the final product. It follows that a lack of sleep coupled with weight gain or weight loss will begin to affect your relationships. And I did say weight loss. Discouragement can cause your weight to go either up or down depending on the kind of physical constitution you have. Also, you will find yourself becoming more defensive in your attitude. You will adopt a combative posture toward those you love the most. There will be more and more occasions when the slightest thing said can be taken the wrong way. All of a sudden you get your feelings hurt a lot easier than ever before, and your tendency to retaliate and hit back becomes a problem. Even your spouse and kids will tell you that you are grumpy and ask, "What's the problem with you?" They'll say, "You need to cheer up," and, "Good grief, don't take it so personal. I was just joking with you!"

4. You could begin to do last-minute preparation for that message you are about to deliver, or that class you are going to teach, or that project you volunteered to undertake. Many people who suffer spiritual burnout are leaders in the spiritual world. They are spiritual leaders at home with their families, they lead their children constantly, they lead at church, and many are leaders in the marketplace. They are always there, front and center. At home they are always teaching, loving, inspiring, and leading. Their home is the center of gravity for all the neighborhood kids. It's the place where all the kids come after the ball game. It's where they all hang out because these are the kind of parents all the kids want to be around. Meanwhile at church they are always available—for everything. They serve in leadership, they teach classes and discipleship groups—often in their homes every week for months and years on end. They serve the youth, the senior adults, the babies, and the kitchen! They sit on committees and always seem to be there when the doors of the church are open. But while all this is going on, a silent killer is at work. Spiritual exhaustion, spiritual burnout!

5. What happens next can be even more subtle than last-minute preparation. It's called taking shortcuts! In a preacher's life this means leaving everything to the last minute to the point at which desperation sets in. And when desperation sets in because time has become a factor, shortcuts begin to look wonderfully attractive. *Let's see what so-and-so has to say on this subject,* he thinks to himself. And so he begins to rely on commentaries and someone else's simple sermon outlines. The Sunday school teacher relegates that preparation time to the last minute and finally resorts to reading from a study book provided by "the agency." And guess what the result is? Boring classes. I had one teacher come to me one time and ask me to pray with him about his class. We talked together, and he told me that things were not the same as they had been for many years. The fizz was going out of his class, and they were no longer growing in any measurable way. I discovered he had been teaching faithfully for many years. He was known as a master teacher by many who had come into real blessing through his life and ministry as a layperson in our church. He was sleep deprived, and this was the result of the long hours he put in at his secular place of work. He was having a tough time on the home front. The love he and his wife shared was beyond question, but he was so busy "serving the Lord" that he certainly spent little time cultivating the romance of his marriage. It had been years since he had taken his wife out on a date. But everybody else thought he was terrific!

We soon discovered that he had increasingly cut back on his preparation time so that he told me he felt more and more unprepared to teach as each Sunday went by. And there it was. The agency manual! The bold letters were emblazoned across the cover, *Teaching Philippians for Teachers.* Now please do not misunderstand me at this point. These teaching aids are wonderful. I am so grateful for agencies like LifeWay Christian Resources in Nashville, Tennessee. We do not need less help. We need more help. And they and others like them do a fantastic job of helping our leaders and teachers understand material and dissect it so that all can hear the wonderful truths of God's Word. But these materials are not meant to be read like a parrot in front of a group of people. If you take the presence and power of the individual personality out of the act of teaching and preaching, something serious is lost.

6. *It soon becomes evident that the compulsion to plagiarize will soon become the order of the day.* Simply copying another's work can be a serious symptom of spiritual burnout. And it really begins as a simple act of desperation. Tomorrow is just around the corner and other people depend on what you have to deliver. Expectations are high, and appreciation levels are already in place. To make matters worse, we are living in a day and age where computers provide easy access to the thoughts and hard work of others. It really is so easy simply to lift another's work and pretend it is your own. But this will catch up. It may go on for a season, but it will come. It is like a drought. As the days turn into weeks, the weeks turn into months; and without rain the trees, bushes, and grass will begin to whither and die! You will just find yourself running out of juice, and then all those who depend on you will begin to slide away.

7. *Deliberate deceit!* The fact is, some people can get so down-and-out they resort to deliberate deceit. This can easily happen when shortcuts lead to plagiarism. There is a

sense in which people can almost become so comfortable in their plagiarizing that they slide into deliberate deceit.

I will always remember one of my seminary professors who told his preaching students a story of horrific proportions. As the pastor of a fine church, he scheduled an annual revival to which he invited a well-known evangelist to be the guest speaker. The first Sunday morning service could not have begun in a more excellent manner. The preacher chose his own personal testimony as the message to kick off the revival. And what a testimony it was, according to our professor. What God had done in the life of this man was too marvelous for words. The congregation was moved to tears. People literally hung on every word. They were rooted to their seats as the speaker shared his story with them. When the invitation was given, scores of people responded. I remember our teacher telling that the rest of the revival week was equally terrific. The church was packed out for every service. Lives were transformed by the power of God. By the time the meeting concluded some days later, the whole church had been greatly blessed and encouraged by all they had seen and heard.

The next year the time came for another revival. The pastor invited a different man of God to come as their guest to lead them to the foot of the cross. Expectations were high, and little advertising was needed because the people were still enjoying the effects of the previous year. But this time things did not get off to a good start. The evangelist stood to deliver the message for the Sunday morning opening revival service and shared that he felt led to share his own personal testimony. You've got it! Within minutes the congregation found themselves listening to exactly the same story they had heard from the man the previous year. It was the same illustrations, same encounters, same sin, and same result. Only this time the man standing before them preached the message as though it had all happened to him. Many people evidently just stood up and walked out of the church in disgust. When the invitation was delivered, not one person responded. The pastor closed the service rather hurriedly and led the guest preacher to an office behind the sanctuary where he told him his obvious deceit would greatly harm the people of his congregation. The visiting preacher bowed his head, as if in prayer, and said, "Well, Pastor, I am so sad to hear about this because the testimony you just heard is my personal testimony. Last year's preacher was the one who deceived you all."

How sad indeed! I have never forgotten the story I heard that day. Things like this, as sad as they are, can be blamed on many things, of course. But it was later discovered that the man who had stolen another's story had gone through the downward cycle of discouragement in his own life. He was one of those men who thought God placed him on this earth to please everybody—other than his own family, that is! And so he spent every waking hour running around at the whim and fancy of everybody else. He just couldn't seem to say no and found himself on the popularity trail desiring affection and approval. He was constantly gone and prided himself on telling everyone just how busy he was and how many meetings he held and that he was basically home only on Fridays each week. "How grateful I am for my wife," he would be heard to say with the genuine belief that this is what constituted a man of God. How foolish!

Before long it all began to catch up with him. Black rings formed under his eyes. He battled going to sleep in motel rooms and soon became one of those men who tell you they have to keep the television going all night "so they can get to sleep." Running from one meeting to another meant that his preparation time began to suffer seriously. He found himself scratching among the chickens to find little morsels of food that someone else had thrown to the ground. He would pick up those morsels and eat them so that he could regurgitate like a cow chewing the cud. It was not too long when he found himself sitting at an evangelism conference listening to the dramatic story of the life and testimony of some other man. When he arrived to begin the revival in this church, he must have thought, *How could anyone in this church ever know this in not my story?* And, then again, the Bible does teach that sin blinds us.

Discouragement always has a beginning. People do not get discouraged for little or no reason. This man had run out of juice. He dried up and desperately needed a good shot of spiritual revitalization.

8. People who become hopeless and discouraged will begin to criticize others. It is part of the cycle. I believe most people who spend time and effort criticizing others are having a crisis themselves. The Bible tells us that the things in the heart will come out of the heart and make themselves known. A critical person is usually someone who is begging for help. Something is gnawing away at them like a cat scratching at the door wanting to be allowed to come inside the home. There are so many jokes that float about concerning those who love to "have church for lunch each Sunday." I recall one sweet lady who came to me privately and reported that her husband was one of those men. She certainly loved him and made clear to me that their marriage was not in danger. But his critical spirit was wearing her down. I simply suggested he was crying out for help. I told her that, in my opinion, a Christian who has a critical spirit has something going on. And he did! And today he is a much happier man.

9. Another effect of spiritual burnout is discontentment. I see this everywhere. Americans are plagued with the spirit of discontentment brought about by extreme materialism. We have it all, folks! Even the most needy in the United States of America have far more than some people in other countries. I have seen some of these people with my own eyes and so have you. It is hard to go on a mission trip to parts of Africa, India, and South America and not be overwhelmed by the pitiful circumstances in which some people find themselves.

Not too long ago my wife and I found ourselves in one of the largest shopping malls in the world. We were in Minneapolis, Minnesota, at a friend's wedding and decided to amble around this mall for a couple of hours. One store

I went into was the Apple Computer store. As I arrived, I found myself stepping over hundreds of people who looked like they were on a camping trip. Some had sleeping bags, others had tents of sorts, and others had chairs and little television sets. Some had food and drinks, and they all looked like they needed a good night's sleep or a jolly good bath! I walked over to one of the workers and asked who these people were and what they were doing sitting on the hard floors of that mall looking like they needed something.

"Oh them," she replied. "Those are people who are waiting for the new iPhones!"

"Are you kidding me," I replied in absolute amazement. "How long have they been out there like that?"

Some of them had been there for two days! What? For an iPhone?

I do not think it is the end of the world for a young person to spend the night in a mall waiting for a new piece of technology (the older folks I'm not so sure about), but think about this with me.

Discouragement will nearly always produce discontentment. And discontentment will nearly always produce discouragement. It works both ways. A person who loses hope and a future thirsts for something they are battling to find. Discontentment is something we are warned about in the New Testament. Paul said, "I don't say this out of need, for I have learned to be content in whatever circumstances I am. I know both how to have a little, and I know how to have a lot. In any and all circumstances I have learned the secret of being content—whether well-fed or hungry, whether in abundance or in need" (Phil. 4:11–12).

This can happen to any of us. Just open your eyes and look around. You will see it everywhere. People want more. They are not satisfied. They want more options, more entertainment, more money, more clothes, more cars, more toys, more things to do, more places to visit, more opportunities, and more things to complain about. Many Christian people spend more time complaining about what they think they need or don't have than thanking the Lord for what they do have. One of my friends who lost a child in an accident said to a group of us who were comforting him, "If I could just have him back here with me, I would never complain about anything again." The truth is, many of us do not know how blessed we really are until it is no longer there. And then it is too late. A spirit of discontentment will leave you spiritually dry and washed out because it is sin against the Lord who has commanded us to be content. Another reason is because your continual negative spirit about where you live and what you eat and who your friends are and what you drive will sap your soul-spirit energy base. It will tap you dry and leave your innermost being dry. Check your spiritual energy level.

9. *Two other serious effects of spiritual burnout are sickness in the body and even the death of the body.* Yes, I'm talking about the things you and I go to the doctor for most of the time and the one thing none of us ever want to think about. Now I realize some may suggest I am getting into a

zone only a doctor is qualified to talk about, but I'm not so sure. Let's start with a passage of Scripture that has always intrigued me.

It has to do with the Lord's Supper. You will remember how the Lord Jesus, on the night before Judas betrayed him, took His disciples into the upper room and served them supper. He gave clear and concise instructions about how to do it and reminded them of the essential meaning and significance of the Lord's table. When the apostle Paul wrote these things, he was careful to outline the meticulous details involved in this wonderful ordinance Christians observe around the world. The part that intrigues me is when Paul warns us about the issue of self-examination:

> Therefore, whoever eats the bread or drinks
> the cup of the Lord in an unworthy way will
> be guilty of sin against the body and blood of
> the Lord. So a man should examine himself; in
> this way he should eat of the bread and drink of
> the cup. For whoever eats and drinks without
> recognizing the body, eats and drinks judgment
> on himself. This is why many are sick and ill
> among you, and many have fallen asleep. If we
> were properly evaluating ourselves, we would
> not be judged. (1 Cor. 11:27–31)

My purpose here is to help you understand the consequences of spiritual burnout. This passage warns us in no uncertain manner as to those consequences. The passage was directed to believers who had polluted the sanctity of the Lord's table by getting drunk because they regarded Communion as an opportunity to drink as much as they wanted of the wine, even to the detriment of those who were poorer and had no wine for themselves. They were guilty of overeating and gluttony because they thought the table was just an opportunity for a feast. Even more seriously, they refused to recognize the spiritual significance of the body and blood of the Lord Jesus Christ and act accordingly.

And so Paul issues a stern warning to them and states categorically that both sickness and death are distinct consequences of their lack of spiritual sensitivity. Death is obviously the extreme form of church purification that the Bible teaches (see Luke 13:1–5; Acts 5:1–11; 1 John 5:16).

Many years ago I was invited to preach a revival in a wonderful church. I arrived to see a brand-new sanctuary and soon learned the revival was the first service held to commemorate its opening to the glory of God. What I did not know was the story surrounding the building of that new sanctuary. The church leadership had evidently made a decision that all the deacons of the church had to be unanimous at every point and stage of the new building. I was told the church body voted to approve the new building, and the deacons determined their unanimity would ensure they would remain on the right track. They were united except for one man. And the more they tried to persuade him, the more he dug in his heels. Months turned into years and still the stalemate continued. Finally, and in a moment of near exasperation, the deacons asked the elderly pastor and one of the deacons to pay this man a visit in his house. Not only did he not want to discuss the matter, but also he took such exception to the pastor coming to his house that he all but physically threw them both out.

The next morning he came down the stairs to have breakfast. His wife said he was looking at her one minute and was stone dead the next!

I have always remembered that revival! One of the extreme consequences of spiritual emptiness is removal. God will not tolerate blood clots in the house of God! The church is the blood flow of the living God. I believe there are many believing but cantankerous men and women that God has removed from the blood flow of His church. I have often wondered where it all began. What I am saying is that your spiritual dryness can have serious consequences. Are you listening to the signs? Do you see anything in your life that is demanding for you to get a spiritual checkup?

I am no expert in these matters, nor do I claim fully to understand these things, but I do know the Word of God tells us that there is a reason some people die. The apostle John calls this "the sin unto death" (see 1 John 5:16–18). What that sin is exactly we do not know because the Bible does not tell us, and maybe it's a good thing we do not know. The fact of the matter is, the Bible says it! Spiritual dryness can be cured, but if it goes on unchecked, it can have dire consequences. I guess this is just like the very difficult issue of suicide. I have personally counseled with grieving people whose lives have been deeply impacted by the suicide of someone they loved. Invariably the families of suicide victims talk about signs and symptoms. But it is too late. Could something have been done to prevent such a radical action?

Early in my ministry I encountered some serious opposition to the work of God in His church. It was obvious to many people that the Lord's hand was being placed on the church in a fresh and vibrant way. I had followed a fine man into the pulpit of one of America's great churches and had been received with open arms and ready hearts, except for a few skeptical people. I did not mind the fact that some people found it hard to adjust to a new pastor, and I certainly recognized that respect is earned by jolly hard work and not by virtue of a position. But one particular man was different. He had been a member of the church for many years and had an axe to grind. Even in my relative inexperience I could see the writing on the wall. I also realized no one in the congregation would stand up to him because of who he was, the family he belonged to, or whatever other reason they could find. He was a blood clot in the house of God. He tried often to get me to engage him, but I had learned never to get in a mud hole with a pig because you will both get covered in mud, and the pig will love it! This man, I feared, was headed for a serious confrontation with God.

One day as I walked into the church, this man yelled out that he wanted to speak to me. My wife just happened to be with me as well as another man in the church. When

I approached him, he told me in no uncertain terms that he had every right as a church member to do anything or get anything he wanted from whoever he wanted. To this day I believe the Lord used me to save his life because I said something to him that grabbed his attention.

I said very politely, "I appreciate all you have to say, but I have one thing I wish to say to you. I have come to the conclusion, after six months as the pastor of this church, that there is not enough room in this church for you and me at the same time, and I am not going anywhere!"

He spluttered a little and then asked me to repeat what I had said. And so I did. "Are you telling me I am going to leave this church after decades of being here?" he inquired with a smirk on his face.

"What I am saying, sir, is this: there is not enough room for you and me in this church, and I am not going any-where. In fact I am happy to tell you just how you are going to leave. The first way could be in a box. I want you to know that I have begun to pray and ask the Lord to cause you to be taken out of this church, if necessary in a coffin. You are the right age to die suddenly. You, sir, are a blood clot in the blood flow of God's house. He will not put up with it, nor will I. We have too much work to do, and there are too many people out there who do not know the Lord Jesus as their personal Savior. Your behavior in church meetings, in the welcome center while worship services are going on, and in general is a discredit to the name of our Savior. And so I'm afraid you must go! The second way, and I trust the preferred way you will leave this church is that you move to some other unfortunate congregation, but I want you to know you will be leaving."

A few months later he left to go to another church.

Another issue brought up by Paul relates to the matter of sickness and pain. It seems evident from his instructions that any believer who fails to examine his or her spiritual standing with the Lord runs the risk of sickness. Now I do not claim to know where headaches, stomachaches, and every other kind of physical ailment come from, but this is what the Bible says. He also talks about weakness as a consequence. I consider this to be somewhat like the spirit of "timidity" or fear that we read about in 2 Timothy 1:7, where Paul says, "For God has not given us a spirit of fearfulness, but one of power, love, and sound judgment." While sickness relates to the physical body, weakness relates to the inner, spiritual body. Roughly translated, this means that the believer who serves the Lord with a spirit of defeatism will be relegated to a life of spiritual fear and timidity. Now what, exactly, constitutes a life of fear for a believer? It's right there in the text. A lack of power, love, and self-discipline! When you loose hope and become discouraged, what are some of the things that begin to vanish in your life. There they are! Your power base begins to fade. This is your God-given ability to stand up and do what you have to do even when you do not feel like it. Your ability to love others with no strings attached begins to go as well. But love begins within you first. It has been said that if you do not love yourself (in the right way), you have little or no chance of being able to love others. Then, of course, you will most certainly not be able to love God. And if you do not love God supremely and love others, you stand in violation of God's essential living commandments. Talk about discouragement!

But don't overlook the element of self-discipline that is essential in the Christian walk. Let's be honest with each other. When you get down in the dumps, one of the things that suffers most is the ability to get things done that need to be done because they are essentials that matter in life. Show me an undisciplined person, and I will show you an unhappy person. When self-discipline goes out the back door, discouragement enters to replace it. Or when discouragement creeps in the front door, self-discipline goes out the back door. In essence your ability to get it all together is removed. It is taken away, and you are rendered impotent and useless.

Let's summarize.

If you are discouraged, something needs to be done to help you. I am suggesting that a good starting point is to check your own spiritual energy level. In other words, how are you doing spiritually? I have outlined a few of the things that could happen to you if, in fact, you have run out of spiritual gas:

1. Disturbed sleep
2. Deprived sleep
3. Physical deterioration

4. Relationship problems
5. Lack of preparation
6. Taking shortcuts
7. Plagiarism
8. Deliberate deceit
9. Critical spirit
10. Discontentment
11. Death
12. Sickness

The question is, what can you do about it? When I realized my spiritual tank was dry, one thing I did was establish a channel of healing for myself. I followed a simple plan. You may want to try this plan that follows:

1. Identify the problem. What exactly is ailing you spiritually?

2. Write it down. I have found that writing these things down is essential to healing and wholeness.

3. Form partnerships. Find a person or persons you can trust to keep and maintain confidences, and share your situation with them. Be frank, open, and honest. The key, of course, is the trust factor. I would caution you to be careful about this. I am constantly shocked and appalled at some people who consider themselves confidants but still feel the compulsion to share private matters with others, often under the guise of a prayer request. Friends who share "prayer requests" with others when they have been told something in confidence grieve the Holy Spirit and damage the one who shared with them. So be careful!

4. *Pray.* Remember Nehemiah! It is not going to happen without prayer. And prayer is probably one of the things you have had to write down because prayer nearly always is one of the first things to suffer when you get down and depressed. This is a tough one because it is difficult to pray when you are down and discouraged.

5. *Develop a clear strategy.* Determine what you are going to do about it. In my case I joined a weekday discipleship group with my wife. Almost every Monday for a year we sat under the teaching of a trained leader in a home with other couples. I was being fed for the first time in years and soon came to realize that I had given out so much but had little coming back in. Little did I realize just how much I needed to be quiet and listen to someone else do the talking.

Set an actual time and place to have a regular quiet time with the Lord. This does not have to be so early in the morning that you sit in a fog. For years I have heard that the only time in the day to have a quiet time with God is before the day begins. I do not believe that to be true because God is not limited by time and space. He is everywhere, all the time. Whatever the time and place, you need a plan that works for you.

6. *Take action.* The water must hit the wheel! Remember that one of the casualties might have been your own self-discipline, and so this one is going to be tough to begin. Get on with it! How many people do you and I know who seem

to spend a lifetime on good intentions, but they never seem to get on with their good intentions.

7. Be accountable. Go back to your partnership group on a regular basis and give an honest account of your status and standing.

When you check your own spiritual energy level, you may be surprised to find the tank empty. Do something about it and see what the Lord will do for you.

Make Sure You Have the Proper Exercise

This is a big one! Before anyone decides to stop reading, please listen to what I have to say. This is so important because you and I know that diet and exercise are either loved or hated. Would you not agree with me that some of the following statements are true?

1. You either love it or hate it!
2. Life's not fair!
3. Skinny people make you want to throw up!
4. Overweight people are stuck in a rut!
5. Millions of pounds are lost every year!
6. Millions of pounds are gained every year!

7. You don't need another program!
8. You have tried and it doesn't work!
9. It's just the way God made you!
10. You would rather be overweight and happy than skinny and unhappy!
11. What are a few more years anyway?
12. You like the way you are!
13. Diets don't work!
14. Just change the subject!

Sounds like you and me, doesn't it? Well it certainly sounds like me. Let me share something with you.

I was born with a kind of "neither here nor there" body. What this means is that most people would look at me and at least think I am pulling their leg when I say that I have a propensity to put on major weight. Many people would possibly regard me as sort of OK when it comes to fat or thin. Until they see me on the beach, that is! I'm OK when all dressed up with a good set of clothes designed to hide what needs to be hidden and accentuate those parts of the body that need to be accentuated. For most of my youth, I battled the bulge. And were it not for an active life, I would have become a little beach ball! But I was into everything and was constantly on the move. My life was outdoors—surfing, swimming, running, and playing every kind of game imaginable. Besides I grew up in the beautiful, wide open, and unhindered spaces of Africa. I had never heard of fast food until I came to America, had never eaten a hamburger until college, had never heard of pizza, and had never eaten in a restaurant until I was in my teens. I remember when "Tiny" came back from America when I was in college and opened a hamburger place in our college town. It was the talk of the town for months on end.

As a result, I was blessed that my childhood and youth were spent relatively free of the junk-food epidemic that has surrounded my kids and yours.

Today is quite different. Food is our pastime and we love it! I certainly do. It is available in every place and has every assortment to offer for every taste. We have so much of it we do not even have to think about where to find food; it's just there waiting to be ordered and eaten. We have so many restaurants to choose from that our kids are even becoming disgruntled because they have so many choices to make. What a blessing we have when so many people around the world have nothing. We not only have hamburgers to eat, but we can choose what kind of hamburger we want. You can get chicken hamburgers, double hamburgers, triple hamburgers, with cheese, fully loaded, without whatever you want without, and add just about anything your heart desires. Your hamburger can be cooked to order—well done, medium, medium well done, cremated, rare, medium rare, or "with just a little pink" on the inside. And, don't forget the fries! While you are at it, get the "biggie" size. And add some onion rings, dipping sauce, and a large cup of sugar. Oops! I mean "sweet tea!"

By the time I was thirty, the front part of my anatomy looked like I had enjoyed every bit of it, and I had!

Traveling to preach and being on the road, I found the convenience of fast food was just that, wonderful and convenient. That was the problem! Then there were the people. Boy! Some of them can cook! I have been to as many dinners-on-the-ground as one could ever imagine, and I have been fed more delicious meals by more precious moms and grandmoms than I could ever say thank you to! Food is part of our social makeup, and it is the place where we do so much visiting together. Besides, it is easier to eat out than in these days.

At the age of thirty-nine, I was called to a most wonderful church in South Carolina. God had certainly blessed my family and me. But with the added responsibilities of a large church came the added stress and all the other things that go along with serving the Lord. My weight situation continued to be a problem a little bit at a time, which meant it was creeping up on me one pound at a time. I went from one fine meal to another, and, were it not for my wife, I might have crashed and burned.

All the while, one of the finest men I have ever met had written me a letter. In the letter he offered to allow me the use of his fitness center, and, more significantly, just offered me loads of encouragement and his personal friendship. John Lankford is that kind of man. Over the years he has never changed for one second. He is a kind and gracious man, but, unfortunately, his letter sat on my desk for a number of years. And, while it did, I continued my downhill slide physically. Here's the point. I now had all I needed to help me, but it just sat there! I did nothing about it! Through John Lankford, God was sending His provision of a place to go and work out, and a well-qualified ear who would lovingly guide and direct me in the area of my physical difficulty. But the letter and His gracious love for me just lay on my desk.

By the time another few years had gone by, several symptoms had made their appearance in my life:

1. Couldn't sleep at night
2. Eating out of control
3. Headaches and other aches out of nowhere
4. Food began to taste "not so good"
5. Extreme tiredness in middle of the day
6. Went to bed tired, woke up tired
7. Clothes felt uncomfortable
8. Did not like myself
9. Became easily angered by silly things
10. Did not want to play with the kids as much
11. Found it harder to concentrate
12. Started joking about my weight
13. Fell into a rut
14. Became more critical of others
15. Drew attention away from my weight by talking too much
16. Seriously discredited my witness for Christ
17. Thought much more about dying suddenly
18. Became increasingly discouraged

19. Thought about leaving the place God had called me to
20. Never wanted to swim at the lake or beach
21. Had to choose frumpy clothes to cover up

One day I woke up and decided I did not want to spend my life like this. I wanted to be there for my wife and kids. I wanted to be alive and make my life count for the Lord Jesus. I wanted my family to be proud of me even though they loved me "just the way I was." The problem was, I did not love myself. I was concerned that I could not be the kind of leader God wanted me to be if my own life was not all it needed to be for the Lord. I knew that my body was the temple of God, and I truly wanted it to be just exactly what it was intended to be.

I went to my friend and confidant, John Lankford. Did you know the Lord will always put precious people in your pathway to help you in every need and circumstance?

John just came alongside me and set a plan out for me. The plan was simple:

1. Go to the gym at least three times a week
2. Change your eating habits

Now let's talk about this. I am a busy man. One of the toughest things for me to do is to go to the gym or fitness center at least three times a week. But this wasn't really a choice. Either do it or suffer the consequences! I had come to the point at which I realized this was something that was a vital part of all that I am. Physical wellness is not an option. It is not an idea that is good for some people and not for others. If you want to do well and feel well, then you have to knuckle down and get on with it. You can't have it both ways. It's like the friend who came to me some years ago and asked me to help him stop smoking.

"Are you really serious about this?" I asked him. He said he was indeed. "Then I'll give you my opinion on how to stop smoking, simply stop!" He looked at me, and I knew exactly what he was thinking, *You foolish man. You obviously do not know what it is like to be totally addicted to cigarettes!*

This is what I told him. "Joe, have you ever tried cutting back before?"

"Yes, I have tried many times," he answered without hesitation.

"Has it worked for you, or are you still hooked on nicotine?"

"No, it has never worked, and I am still as hooked as I have ever been."

"OK, then," I continued, "here's what will happen if you just lay those smokes down and make a decision, with the Lord's help, to quit. At first you will be OK for about a day or so. Then you will start going through the worst kinds of withdrawal imaginable. This won't be easy at all. You might shake, throw up, feel like you are being slowly strangled to death, or any number of awful reactions. But slowly and surely, your body will adjust to the change that is taking place. And it will be worth the pain because you will be set free from this thing that has you in its grip."

My friend did exactly as I had suggested. He went through the worst kinds of pain but came out the other side and has not touched a cigarette in more than six years now.

Now my slide into a negative physical condition was by no means as drastic as my friend's predicament with cigarette smoke. But it had me in its grip. I was overeating, under-sleeping, and quietly slipping into a depression spiral.

My first visits to the fitness center were a nightmare. I felt as though everyone was staring at me, even though they were not. The place was full of people just like me. We were all puffing and panting, and we were all cheering one another onwards and upwards. If you have a picture in your mind of me lifting weights and bouncing off the walls, you are seriously misinformed. Most of what I did centered on aerobics and walking on a treadmill. John helped me go through the different exercise stations so that I was able to start off gently. And the first couple of times I went, I felt like throwing up afterwards—and did on one occasion! But I soon found a rhythm and never looked back.

The second issue related to my diet—what I ate! I love food; it's as simple as that. And to make matters even more complicated, a great deal of my work and ministry revolves around food because I am in the people business. I wish I could tell you that I never pig out and eat everything that's offered, but I can't. However, I am so much more conscious of what I eat these days. I try to eat less of a portion of food, and I try seriously to limit myself when it comes to the "deadlies." Some of the deadlies for me are breads, anything fried, sugars and sweets, anything white like white rice and white baked potatoes, and so on. I have just switched to many more salads, fish, chicken (all grilled), sweet potatoes, and the like.

Now that a number of years have passed by, I wish I could invite you to come and take a good look at me. I certainly wish I could report to you that I have the most fantastic physique in South Carolina, but I cannot! I still battle with overeating and a lack of sleep. I still work long hours and destroy all my hard work over one large chocolate malted milk shake from Brewster's from time to time because I just have to be hospitable to my friends and a true daddy to my daughter!

But there is a difference. Here it is. The cobwebs are gone!

I believe that people who are out of shape have what I call "cobwebs" in their heads. And I have also learned that being skinny is not necessarily a sign that you are healthy. Many fine looking people have a constitution that accommodates a lot of junk food, but it is what is on the inside that really counts. When you have just a little exercise, like taking a walk, and when you control your eating habits, you will be amazed what a difference it makes. The days will look brighter. You will be able to sleep better and work harder. And you will find that you are able to make better decisions at work, home, and play. When you need to focus on a project, you have a greater ability to shut out distractions, and, when you go to church, you will actually be able to listen and absorb all the Lord is saying to you instead of sitting there and just looking like you are paying attention.

General physical wellness is crucial to good living, and you do not want to go through life cheated out of the best God has intended for you. You can do something about it! Perhaps the reason you are so discouraged is because you desperately need to check your physical energy level. Just do it! It's worth it. Go and find a friend, your John Lankford. Precious people like John are out there. And besides, God cares about you and will help you. Make a start and watch what happens. You will be amazed at the difference it will make in your entire life. Everything you do and say will be affected by it!

Chapter Three

Spend Time with Someone Who Is Not Discouraged

This may sound a little corny and maybe a little simplistic, but I could not be more serious about this wonderful means to overcome discouragement. In my own personal life I cannot tell you the number of times God has sent along the right person at the right time to help bring me back into focus and reality.

My life as a pastor is absolutely wonderful. I still cannot truly believe the Lord has allowed me the honor and privilege of serving a wonderful group of people. But it is still hard work. Now I want you to think about something you may not have thought about. Pastors have to be careful about the looks on their faces. Just imagine that I arrived at church on a Sunday morning for worship to find the place packed out with expectant people. Let's imagine that I've been up all night with a sick child at home and then called out to help a family in need. Just imagine if I then stood before the people and said something like this, "Well folks, I feel pretty awful this morning, and quite frankly I don't really feel like being here today. But I guess I have to be here, so why don't you take out your Bible and let's get this over with!" This certainly has the promise of a fine worship encounter!

This is not to suggest that pastors are not entitled to feel down like any other normal person, but my personal conviction remains that as long as I am with people and serving the Lord, I have no right ever to be down in public because my long face just might be a means of discouragement to someone needing encouragement. My practice has always been that if I am not feeling up to it, then it is far better to stay at home and get well. All people understand what it means to get sick.

This is where some special people come into the picture. God always seems to place such people around those who need them most. Here are some of the ways you can spot a person who is not discouraged:

1. They have a smile on their faces.
2. They have a positive reputation.
3. Their eyes seem to sparkle when they look at you.
4. They have a precious disposition.

5. They are not known for being down on everything.
6. They are true servants.
7. Nothing is ever too much trouble for them.
8. Kindness seems to flow from them.
9. God draws your attention to them.

If you are serious about becoming an overcomer, just open your eyes and look around. You can spot them in a minute. But the truth is, you probably know who they are already. It's that precious lady who always has the time to go up to people and say a kind word to them. It's that grandfather who always seems to be more interested in what others are doing than in his own circumstances and affairs. It's that teacher you know; it's that person you just gravitate toward. Go to them. Sometimes you don't even have to say anything. They know already without your having to say one word. They know because God has given them a special intuitive gift whereby they are able to discern your need. The thing about these special people is that you don't even have to tell them all about it; they are willing just to be there for you. They will let you know that you don't have to spill it all out unless you want to!

Go and find that someone who is not discouraged, and you will be surprised what will happen. You will be blessed indeed!

Chapter Four

Do Something
for Someone Else

One of the greatest and most effective ways of releasing the discouragement in your life is to do something for someone else. One of the many consequences of discouragement is that you begin to look inward instead of outward. In a sense you become hyper-selfish because your world revolves around you. The more down in the dumps you are, the more you will be inclined to implode on yourself. I have watched fine Christian people go through this many times. Unfortunately I have watched some people move from the front of the church, to the middle of the church, to the back of the church, and out to the street that runs by the church. Please stay connected when you are going through a hard time. The pain will try to make us close ranks on ourselves. We become so hurt that we become embarrassed by our hurt and pain. We run away instead of staying and allowing those who love us most to help us through our difficulties.

Now, what do you suppose this kind of isolation produces? Selfishness. And the more selfish you become, the more discouraged you become because being self-centered is not the way God created us to behave.

I have discovered one of the most effective ways to overcome this malady. Do something for someone else! It's the law of the Bible that teaches two essential principles in this regard:

1. It is more blessed to give than it is to receive.
2. If you sow generously, you will reap generously.

These two principles provide us with a way out from our discouragement. They will liberate our discouragement-captured hearts. Discouragement is nothing short of captivity because it progressively holds us in its grip. The more discouraged, the tighter the grip; and the tighter the grip, the more discouraged we become. Giving to others is a way of liberating our souls.

I am convinced this is what happened to Karyn and me in the early days of our life in America. Not that I would suggest we "had it all" when we were both schoolteachers in Africa, but we were fairly comfortable. Both of us taught school. We had an adventurous and exciting early life together. Our days were filled with sporting activities, beaches and surf, motorbikes and family time. It was great but awfully selfish when I look back on that time. I had not yet learned this lesson of giving. Most things revolved around yours truly, me. I did not understand that God uses people to bless other people. I had not learned about being God's instrument of blessing to others and regarded myself as the center of my own universe.

This selfishness carried over into my marriage. I hurt my beautiful bride terribly with my self-centeredness. She was devoted to loving and providing for me. I was devoted to loving me and providing for me. My world simply and sadly revolved around me.

Then the Lord called us into full-time Christian ministry. For us it was a radical change from all we knew. We had to give up our joint incomes, our home, our family, and our country. Karyn sold most of her possessions and wedding gifts in order to pay off our government loans and buy the tickets necessary to travel to New Orleans for seminary.

Our first few months were a wonderful adventure, but they were extremely hard in many ways. People were kind to us. We were given a small one-room efficiency apartment on the beautiful campus of New Orleans Baptist Theological Seminary. We had almost nothing. We had two suitcases with some meager possessions, but we had no money. I mean *no* money! Some people who say they have no money actually mean they have a little here and there that they cannot touch for some reason. We could not touch it because there was none. I am telling you this not as a sob story but as a testimony to the faithfulness of the Lord who never lets us down.

There we were in a strange city—no money, no family. This was a prescription for discouragement and depression. Karyn and I had grown up on the beautiful Indian Ocean, and here we were in New Orleans! Please understand. I love the city of New Orleans. My three children were born there, and my two sons, Rob and Greg, live there today. I even love the New Orleans Saints. But let's face it, even though it has a French name, New Orleans is not the French Riviera!

One Monday morning Karyn and I woke up and realized we did not have enough money even to buy a doughnut to eat. So we just loved on each other a little and waited. We didn't have to wait long because a knock on the door presented us with a gentleman from Mississippi who said he had heard about us and wondered if he and his wife could take us out to lunch. I tried to be cool, calm, and collected so as not to reveal the rumble in my stomach. How precious they were to us. I can still remember that meal. I ordered the number 9 "Gunsmoke" steak. When they dropped us off at our apartment, the man left a one hundred dollar bill in my hand. Wow! A million dollars to me! When I showed it to my wife, she said, "Oh! This is too wonderful. God is so good. Now we can take this money and go and give it to that couple who live in the Willingham apartments who have nothing!"

"What?" I responded, "Have you lost your mind?"

"No," Karyn said, "the best thing we can do with what we have been given is to give it away."

I can still see myself placing the money in an unmarked envelope and slipping it under the door of the couple Karyn had in mind.

When we returned to our place, I opened the door to find an unmarked envelope under our doorway with two hundred dollars inside!

I have again never doubted God's principles of giving. Part of the motto of my life has been "Now it's my turn!" because God has proved this principle to me time without number. And the most significant impact of giving to someone else is deliverance from the scourge of discouragement and depression.

Give it away! Give it away! So many people are stingy with their possessions. And one of the consequences of being stingy is that it steals our hope and our future. If you want to be set free from inner bondage, do something for someone else. And this is not limited to money, although money is often the issue. I knew a wealthy man who grew tomatoes. They were the best. He would often come by and give us loads of them, and we were grateful. But sometimes it's not tomatoes people need!

When did you last dig into your own pocket for another person? Here's the acid test. Ask yourself these six questions about your giving, and you will soon find out whether or not you are on the right track with God.

1. Is it genuine? Does your giving come from your heart or from your head? Genuineness defines the quality of your soul-spirit as you give. Jesus said, "Give, and it will be given to you; a good measure—pressed down, shaken together, and running over—will be poured into your lap. For with the measure you use, it will be measured back to you" (Luke 6:38). What Jesus was talking about is the matter of ratio and proportion. While the matter of quantity is unimportant, the matter of quality is vitally important. It is the quality of your heart that counts in God's economy. Are you giving from a genuine heart that wants to honor the Lord and serve others, or are you giving from a sense of duty or expectation of self-gain?

2. Is it sacrificial? Here again we have to understand that giving God's way is not about equal giving; it is about equal sacrifice. It would be ludicrous to think all people are able to give the same amount to the Lord's work. When challenged about giving, King David replied, "I will not offer to the LORD my God burnt offerings that cost me nothing" (2 Sam. 24:24).

Wow! So the question we need to ask ourselves is whether or not our giving costs? I think the reason is because God will not accept a tip from us. Many Christians simply tip God. They fumble around and give a little bit here and a little bit there whenever it is suitable. Ask yourself some of the following questions, and you will soon determine whether or not your giving is sacrificial:

- Do you only give when asked?
- Do you usually wait for someone to approach you with a formal request?
- Do you love to weigh your options?
- Do you prefer to have your name recognized when you give?
- Do you insist on retaining control once you have given to a bona fide organization?
- Do you get mad when things are not done the way you like it to be done and then ask for your money back?
- Do you give because of personalities involved or the mission for which the money is given?
- Do you really trust God to honor your giving?
- Do you give with no strings attached?
- Do you give and hurt a little when you do?

3. *Is it responsible?* Responsible giving pleases the heart of God. This basically boils down to the old question, "Am I my brother's keeper?" Yes, you are! Jesus said we must love Him with all our hearts and then we must love our neighbor as we love ourselves. Responsibility in giving is a certain indicator of the manner with which I accept the role and privilege God has given me in this world. Because you are given much, God requires you to shoulder much! The more you have, the more you are required by God to give to others. A major source of discontentment and discouragement comes from the lack of responsible giving.

4. Is it trustworthy? Can God trust you with money and possessions? The measure of that trust is in proportion to the manner with which you give. And this includes just about anything; cars, homes, vacation homes, resources, influence, leadership, and the list goes on.

I think this is true of most things we have been blessed with. There is a direct correlation between the manner with which we give and the heart with which we operate. Many selfish people are a bunch of grumpy old men! Just look at the misers of the world. Many times they are anything but contented and happy. Their lives seem to be wrapped up in themselves. Many of them are suspicious of others, complain and criticize a great deal, and are constantly looking for more. The old saying that "money cannot buy happiness" is so true. Conversely, I personally know many people who have been blessed in many ways and are some of the happiest and most contented people I know. Usually the key is their open hearts and pocketbooks. There seems to be a direct correlation between a giving heart and a happy heart. A heart that gives sacrificially is a blessed heart indeed!

5. Is it cheerful? Have you ever been given something reluctantly! It's like going to a restaurant and ordering your favorite meal, but then the waiter comes and hands you your meal with a bad attitude attached. My daughter and I had a wonderful weekend together in New York City some time ago. We decided to dine in the section known as Little Italy. The food was wonderful, but our problem was the waiter. The good food was spoiled by his bad attitude.

Just think about this for a minute. Jesus made the point of telling us that God loves a cheerful giver. Perhaps another way of saying this is, God expects a giver to be cheerful when he gives! Otherwise it is not a sweet aroma to Him. This does not mean that giving has to be done with a smile on the face. Rather the mandate here is a mandate of the heart once again. Here are some tests for the cheerfulness of your heart as you give:

- Do you give with reluctance in your heart?
- Do you give with resistance in your heart?
- Do you give with reservations in your heart?
- Do you give with requirements in your heart?

How do you measure up? Perhaps this is a major reason you are struggling so much with yourself and everything you are doing. Remember, it is more blessed to give than to receive. But you can give it all away and yet still not be free because your heart is stopped up. Talk to the Lord about this and open your heart as you give. Take your hands off of it and hand it over. If you give a hamburger to a drunk and he walks out the door and dumps it in a garbage can because he just wanted money from you, then so be it. You have done what is right in the sight of God. You do not have to be in control of your stuff because it really is not your stuff. It all belongs to the Lord, and He has just loaned it to you in the first place. And besides, you are not going to take it with you when you go to heaven. So let it go with a cheerful heart while you still have the opportunity to do so.

You may remember when the billionairess Leona Helmsley died. She left five million each to two of her grandchildren, twelve million to her dog, and nothing to two other grandchildren! The two favored grandchildren were required to visit the monument erected in honor of her son, their father, on the anniversary of his death in order to validate the five million they had been granted. How sad indeed! And how sad to think there are Christian men and women who know and love the Lord but conduct their affairs in much the same way as a lady, who from most indications, did not have a personal relationship with the Lord Jesus.

6. *Is it responsive?* There is a difference between responsible giving and responsive giving. Both are essential mandates of giving, but responsive giving is giving that comes from two sources: an open heart and open eyes. We have talked about the importance of having an open heart. But if your eyes are closed to the needs of the world around you, then you are not placing yourself in a position to see the need. Our world is screaming for help, and people are desperate everywhere. My two sons, Rob and Greg, are being used mightily of the Lord in the city of New Orleans. Rob once pointed out to me that it always saddened him to hear people talk about the unreached people groups of the world and yet never seem to realize that the city of New Orleans contains one of the most significantly lost group of people in the world. As much as I love the Crescent City, I must agree with my son. There you have

an excellent example of just how serious cultural religion can blind a people and justify their sinfulness. Even the world famous king cakes that are so much a part of Mardi Gras are designed around Christian themes and symbols. The little plastic baby is actually the baby Jesus, but no one would know this. The colors that decorate the cake are the colors of the gold and frankincense and myrrh that the three kings brought to the newborn baby in the manger, but few people would know this.

When your heart is open and your eyes are open, you will see the crowds. You will see the needs. God will stir your heart and drive you to give. And when you do give in response to needs, you will be released and set free from an inner bondage. The joy you will experience will unravel your predicaments and liberate the emotional noose around your neck. Your giving will have a newfound purpose, and God will bless you in the deepest parts of your soul. Some of the happiest people I know are those who walk into my office and simply say, "Pastor, I am sure that family must need a little help. Would you take this gift and give it to them. And, by the way, I don't want them to know it came from me." "Well, how did you know they had a need?" I may ask. "I've just noticed they seem to be struggling. They drive that old car and I just feel like they need some extra help."

Try this approach. Simply talk to the Lord about it. Ask Him to open your eyes to see the need. When you become spiritually aware, you will respond from your heart. And when this happens, a joy will flood your life like never before.

Giving is the window of your heart. It is the expression of your soul. It is accompanied by God's promise to bless. A discouraged person needs to know of God's blessings. It's yours for the doing!

One of my most significant life lessons on giving happened early in my career while Karyn and I lived on the campus of the New Orleans Baptist Theological Seminary. God had called us to enter full-time Christian ministry, and we were surrounded by an incredible faculty, staff, and more of God's grace than we could ever have deserved. One Friday night we gathered at the apartment of some friends with one purpose in mind, to have some fun with our young families. Before long Dave and I determined to make a quick run to the local supermarket to buy as much junk food as possible. It was rather late in the evening, but we went anyway. This was an adventurous time of our lives, but as I look back, I must admit it was a difficult time for us. We were learning to "walk by faith and not by sight," which is easier said than done. Our finances were just about nonexistent; we were traveling from here to there preaching the Word of God, and I was trying to make ends meet by working as a painter in the maintenance department of the seminary.

And so off we toddled to the grocery store to stock up on snacks and things. As we prepared to leave the store, I could not help but notice a couple standing in line. I guess my eyes were open at that stage of my life. I knew my heart was open. There they were. Right in front of me stood a couple with a small child who were in dire straights. They had bought just one small carton of milk and a small box of doughnuts.

Dave and I quickly paid the cashier and headed for the door. But as we approached the door to the grocery store, we both suddenly stopped and looked at each other. "Are you thinking what I'm thinking, Dave?" I asked. He nodded his head. "OK, here's what we are going to do. Whatever I have in my wallet I am going to give to that couple. What about you?" When I opened my wallet, the consternation on my face told the story. I had forgotten I had put about one hundred dollars, which was a lot of money to us, in the back flap of my wallet just that afternoon. So I suggested we give Dave's money! Just kidding. Dave gave me his money, and I took both our shares of the gift and approached the couple from behind, which is not usually a good idea in New Orleans late at night!

"My friend, please do not turn around. A friend and I just wanted to give you a gift to help you and your family. Please know the reason we are doing this is because the Lord Jesus lives in our hearts. I want you to know that the Lord Jesus Christ has made all the difference to me. He's my best friend, and He wants to be your best friend as well. What He has done for me, He will do exactly the same for you!"

And, with that, I turned and hurried out of the store. That evening we had a wonderful time with our families.

I am not sure I thought about that poor couple in any significant way after that night.

Until about eight years later, that is. At that time I was privileged to serve as a professor on the faculty of New Orleans Baptist Theological Seminary. Early one semester I was asked to preach in chapel. After my message I walked down the platform stairs for the traditional handshakes and comments. When the line had run out, a well-dressed young man was looking me square in the eyes.

"You don't remember me, Dr. Wilton?" he queried warmly. I shook my head politely. "Well, please let me tell you my story.

"About eight years ago my life came to an end. I lost my job and my respect. My wife could not find work, and we became destitute. It became so bad that we decided to make a suicide pact to end our lives. The problem was our little girl. We decided to drive down to New Orleans and jump off a bridge taking our little girl with us. We could not allow her to be left behind in this cruel and unforgiving world. We chose New Orleans because we knew it would be no big deal, just another death. As we drove over the high-rise in east New Orleans, we ran out of gas. We coasted down the Louisa Street exit and just made it to a large grocery store parking lot. My wife looked at me and said she did not want our little girl to die hungry. So we counted up all the money we had left. Merely enough change to buy some milk and a few doughnuts to fill her little tummy. Our plan was to walk back up the high-rise and then jump together into the black hole below. As we were about to pay, a man walked up behind me and stuck nearly two hundred dollars under my arm. He told me he was doing this because Jesus lived in his heart.

"I was stunned. We got back into our car and sat there for hours just crying our eyes out. Early in the morning we decided we could not go through with our suicide pact. And, besides, we now had enough money to get a tank of gas and head back up the interstate to Alabama. Slowly our lives began to come back together. One Sunday morning we were walking past a church and heard them singing about 'the friend we have in Jesus.' I told my wife, 'Remember, that's what that man said to us in New Orleans.' So we went inside the church and ended up giving our hearts and lives to the Lord Jesus. I managed to find a reasonable job, and we began a new life together with the Lord Jesus living in our hearts. About six months ago we realized the Lord was calling us into Christian ministry, but I had not even gone to college. Our pastor told us we could go to New Orleans Seminary and study for a college degree even though I was older than twenty-five. We have just arrived on this campus, Dr. Wilton, and this is the first chapel service I have attended. When you stood up and began to speak, I immediately recognized that accent."

Wow!

I will never forget this important lesson of life. God not only expects us to give it away, but giving something to someone else is an essential antidote to discouragement and despondency.

What have you done lately?

Chapter Five

Simplify Your Life

One of the many problems people face in today's world is the curse of busyness. We live in a fast-paced world, and it shows little sign of letting up and slowing down.

In many households, both parents work outside the home. Fewer mothers stay at home and devote all their time and energy to their children and their families. Sadly, many of these mothers have to work just to make ends meet. But many do not have to work outside the home. The only reason they are out there is because they want to have more and do more. I am not trying to be judgmental, but facts are facts. Whereas the senior generation of people tended to be builders, the baby boomers tend to be hoarders and accumulators. We want more, we want it better, and we want it now! We also want to provide well for our children.

So here we are now as parents. Some of us work multiple jobs in order to survive while others work equally hard in order to have more. In both instances, the soil is a fertile breeding ground for discouragement and depression. I have heard it said that when we balance the three biggies in our lives—work, church, and family—there is not much time left over for anything or anyone else. Honestly, we don't have time to cultivate true and meaningful friendships with other people even though this is so important to a sense of well-being.

The balancing act is all too true today. How do we balance all the things we need to do and the places we need to be with the need to keep in shape and the need for recreation? One young mother simply burst into tears when she spoke to me about her exhaustion level. She had a full-time job outside the home, two small children juggled between grandma's home and a day-care service, and her husband continually trying to get home early. This mother could not even have a lunch break while at work because she had to run home to check on the children. When she did get back home, she found herself confronted by multiple things needing her attention. Just getting the kids to bed is a full-time occupation alone! Needless to say they did not have time to cook meals at home too often, and so they settled into that wonderful American convenience of "I'll just pick up something on the way home from work, honey." When they went out to eat, which was frequent, the best place to go was McDonald's because it provided a play area for the kids. This was good for parents too exhausted to deal with kids in a restaurant while also trying to carry on an adult conversation. McDonald's gave them an opportunity to look when "Watch me, Daddy" came from within the maze of excited kids running back and forth between mouthfuls of French fries washed down with gulps of Coke.

What do you suppose the short- and long-term results are for this family? It all starts out innocently enough, but it soon catches up. It cannot be avoided.

Here comes the clinch! This couple truly loves the Lord Jesus. No doubt about it! Their church occupies a very important place in their lives. Their heart's desire is to bring up their children in the knowledge and admonition of the Lord. They believe strongly in the motto, "The family that goes to church stays together." As a result they are faithful in every way. Not only are they faithful in service; they are faithful in giving and faithful in attendance. They have willing hearts to serve in any capacity and so are frequently approached and asked to host children's events, serve as team and committee members, and to be front and center at almost everything that takes place at church. They are the kind of couple whose advice is sought and whose presence is desired.

So what should they do? Discouragement is a "creepy" thing. It slowly creeps up and sneaks up, and many do not realize what is going on until it is too late. Before long nothing ever seems to get accomplished. When life begins to pile up, it turns into garbage. And piled up garbage can really smell after a while. The solution is simple. Do something about it. Otherwise you will be caught in a quagmire of discontent.

This cycle of discontentment begins innocently.

Step 1: "I must provide" is the given mind-set. No one can argue with basic necessity. Marriage brings responsibility, and responsibility demands provision. Any decent parent will do whatever it takes to provide for the needs of the family.

Step 2: At least the kids have good clothes now! Thousands of parents justifiably derive great satisfaction when their family members are well taken care of. Believe me I know what it is like to go to school dressed in secondhand clothes, hand-me-downs, and mission-box designers! I was fortunate enough to go to schools where uniforms were the order of the day. At least we all looked alike. Today's kids are in a high state of competition from start to finish, especially the girls! And it doesn't stop when the kids go off to college, either.

Step 3: This is what we do. The baby boomer generation seems convinced that their calling in life is to make certain their children need nothing. And should they need anything at all, it is not the child's responsibility to go out and work for it. That's what parents are for.

The result of all this chaotic desire to provide the best of the best and the most of the most is that many parents are flat-out depressed and discouraged. And it doesn't stop when the kids leave home. More and more of our kids graduate from college without any real mission and purpose in life and simply come back home. There are many good reasons for this, I am certain. No loving parent would turn a son or daughter away, but many kids just come back home because they can get all their needs met. Many young men and women in their twenties still do little to make a living for themselves. Most parents would never admit this, but having a grown child occupying the house with little purpose is like a fog. Who would want to say that to a son or daughter? So the choice becomes no choice at all. Just live with it. It's what you do.

Step 4: I'm stuck! Many of these people find themselves stuck. It reminds me of that well-known advertisement of the old lady who took a tumble and said, "Help, I've fallen, and I can't get up!"

Step 5: Life stinks. Now what more needs to be said about this quandary? All previous plans and aspirations get laid aside. Included in these plans are those designed to help us breathe again. We plan to reorganize our homes, put away all the old stuff, get the family pictures in order, write that book, and travel together. But these tasks are seldom accomplished. How depressing!

The family begins disintegrating one step at a time. Before they realize it, the water is at boiling point. The children become increasingly irritable and want more of whatever it is they want. Parents simply give in and capitulate because they really don't want to create a scene, especially at McDonald's or at church. They resort to feeding them endless amounts of sugar as a desperate means to placate and silence them. Discipline takes a decisive backseat! Mom and Dad begin to pick at each other, then argue and eventually fight. They go to bed more and more with feelings of anger and hostility in their hearts. He insists on watching television until late at night, and she gets back at him by keeping the reading light on so she can systematically page through another of those wonderful magazines that present nothing more than a world of fabricated make-believe. His world of fabricated make-believe is his work, and when he is not at work or ordering a fresh round of French fries at McDonald's, he's sitting on a couch or chasing his football team around the nation. He begins to believe that football teams actually define a full and meaningful life. Besides it gets him out of the house, and that enables him to survive what has become a war zone. In the middle of all of this, both Mom and Dad gradually get out of shape and don't really care! The more the weight piles on, the more unhappy they become. Romance takes a leave of absence, and the marriage bed becomes almost nonexistent. The last time they went on a date is almost laughable, and they soon settle into a rut of utter helplessness. At first they become discouraged. Then they become disillusioned. Then they become depressed. The ugliness starts—the talk, the accusations, the suggestions—and the downhill slide is well on its way out the door!

Whew! Sounds tough, and even a little harsh, doesn't it? But this is reality. Scenes and scenarios like this are unfolding like chairs being put out for a massive concert in a park.

The bottom line is that nothing is being accomplished even though one would think, by all appearances, that much is being accomplished. Allow me to suggest a nine-point approach that may help you start getting your life back in order:

1. Admit you have a problem.
2. Write down everything you are doing.
3. Confide in one person you can trust completely.
4. Present everything to the Lord.
5. Set a time of prayer and fasting.
6. Order your list by priority.
7. Eliminate from the bottom up.
8. Focus time and energy from the top down.
9. Accomplish one task at a time in order of priority.

This is simply a plan of action. You may well develop a far better plan. I encourage you to do it. It's not the plan that is important. It's the fact you have a plan that's important.

Six Essential Questions of a Workable Plan

1. Is it totally honest?
2. Is it absolutely complete?
3. Is it able to be carried out?
4. Is it capable of being evaluated?

5. Is it designed to make a difference?
6. Is it inclusive of all who are affected by it?

Pose these six questions once you have outlined your plan of action. The big one, always, is the need to eliminate the things you do from the bottom up. Remember, it does not mean the items on the bottom half of your list are necessarily bad or illegitimate. On the contrary, they may well be good and essential. But you cannot do everything! Neither can I. Trying to say no and order one's priorities is tough. But you know as well as I that the busier you become the less effective you become. Your mind begins to fog up and get so cluttered that you cannot be your best and do your best. Many times it is not only your family that will suffer but also your work, and everything else starts to go on a rapid decline. Before long you become frustrated, then discouraged, and eventually depressed. So settle this once and for all. You can do something about this, but you must take action to simplify your life. It does no good to keep on thinking about it and doing nothing about it. You will discover that, once you have determined to accomplish a task and do it well, you will receive an impetus like never before. Fuel will flow into your tank again. You will suddenly rediscover yourself and have a renewed sense of purpose, energy, and power.

Chapter Six

Be a Witness

Most Christians will readily agree that sharing one's faith in the Lord Jesus is an indispensable mandate from the heart of God Himself. The Great Commission lays this mandate down in no uncertain terms:

> Go, therefore, and make disciples of all nations,
> baptizing them in the name of the Father and
> of the Son and of the Holy Spirit, teaching
> them to observe everything I have commanded
> you. (Matt. 28:19–20)

Jesus repeatedly issued the challenge to witness. Throughout His ministry He presented His disciples their marching orders, and I believe He wanted them to know that Christians who fail to witness would be rendered weak and impotent in living their lives to the fullest. Witnessing to others, soul winning, not only results in joy, but it emboldens the Christian walk. It fortifies our personality and develops Christian character. It's like the saying, "The more you walk, the more you talk; and the more you talk, the more (you are able) to walk."

But witnessing to others is a little like that first girl a young man notices. She captures his attention, and he desires to get to know her. The hardest part is that first conversation. But as soon as he "plucks" up the courage to walk up to her and begin to talk to her, he will never look back.

So it is with sharing Jesus with others. Shyness, fear, laziness, apathy, or whatever can be roadblocks. Most Christians who never or seldom share their faith are people who may love the Lord but struggle to stand up straight in the difficulties of this world.

I have always loved the many stories and events that surrounded the Sea of Galilee. The place itself speaks of a fountainhead or a springboard to life. Known as one of the most fertile regions in the land of Israel, the Galilee has always been a key producer of fruit. Most people who travel there thoroughly enjoy the magnificence of the greenery and the freshness of the air. Perhaps it is little wonder that our Savior sailed the sea many times and called so many of His disciples to forsake all and follow Him from those very shores. When Jesus issued His call to "follow Me," He quickly added "and I will make you fishers of men." That is the heartbeat of witnessing and soul winning. Witnessing is a key ingredient to overcoming discouragement. I personally do not believe the act of soul winning to be something naturally done by most believers. The overriding presupposition made by many continues to place emphasis on the few who, somehow, have been especially selected by the Lord for this specific assignment. Some even incorrectly associate the "gift of an evangelist" spoken of by Paul in his letter to the Ephesians, to be the overriding excuse for most believers to avoid Jesus' mandate to witness.

Foundations of Soul Winning

There are six foundations of soul winning established by the Lord Jesus when He called those men to follow Him. These include the *who*, the *when*, the *how*, the *whom*, the *what*, and the *where* of soul winning. Let's look at the who and the when:

1. The Who. The personal pronoun *I* says it all! Jesus Christ is the centerpiece of soul winning. He is the focus of soul winning. He is the subject of soul winning. He is the sole substance of soul winning. It begins with Him and it ends with Him. When our attention is not placed squarely on the Lord, we begin to focus on ourselves. And when we see ourselves, fear takes control. I am convinced that the number one deterrent to soul winning is fear. Many people are simply afraid of the whole thing. Minds run rampant when the subject is broached. Many fine people are afraid of what might happen to them if they opened their mouths. Many people would rather swim the English Channel during the dead months of winter than share their faith with another person. When the Lord Jesus told the men He would be the one, He was telling them He would be the instigator, the initiator, and the enabler of all that is involved in being a witness. In a sense He was saying, "Leave it up to Me."

Perhaps we have become so wrapped up in techniques and training that we have neglected the person and work of our Savior. Every program and workshop I have been a part of has been helpful in equipping me and others to become more effective as soul winners, but I cannot loose sight of the *who* of witnessing.

2. The When. The next segment of Jesus' statement contains a tense. "Will" points to the future but not as an opportunity to come or as a possibility to consider. The verb tense by no means removes the imperative mandate from the instruction of the Lord Jesus. Rather, I believe, the tense refers to the wonderful process of Christian discipleship. Growth and maturation remain key ingredients of this process. While the "will" places an emphatic insistence on the imperative, the idea lends itself to cultivation and potential. The fertile region of the Galilee must have spoken volumes to the men who followed him as raw recruits on that day. Just as seeds are sown and planted, so the Lord Jesus was telling the men that their obedience in following Him by forsaking all was just the seed, only the beginning of the

Christ life. Just as the cultivated seed produces a harvest (in the future), so the Lord Jesus "will" be the one "who" will enable His followers to become "fishers of men."

Soul winning is an activity that must always be grown and cultivated in the lives of every believer. Believers who claim to love Christ and yet will not fish for men inevitably have a huge emptiness in their hearts and lives. I am convinced that many believers battle with discouragement because they are not sharing their faith with others.

I will admit this is a constant challenge in my own personal life. Many times I zone out of witnessing, and I have every excuse known to man. Busyness tops my list. I am too busy preaching, pastoring, visiting, organizing, and playing to be engaged in this soul-food activity. But what I find is that my own soul is strengthened and my own disposition is warmed when I actively share my faith with others. My attitude improves, and a fresh spark comes into my eye. But when I am lazy and negligent, so many other little things seem to bear down on me. The sideshows of life take center stage. My focus is out of focus, and my affections become misplaced.

The truth, though, is that few of us are actually willing to go out and witness! Our churches have fallen asleep at the wheel, and it should be of little surprise that so many church fellowships have run out of gas. Take a look around and see it for yourself. Churches are dying all around us, and many worship services have been reduced to humdrum presentations of the "same old same old." It should be of little wonder that fewer numbers of young people are gracing the doors of our churches.

The Lord taught me a wonderful lesson some years ago. You may remember the terrible disaster that occurred in Grand Forks, North Dakota, in 1997. The river that runs through the city flooded, resulting in unmitigated disaster for many of the residents.

The Billy Graham Evangelistic Association invited me to join with a team of their people to go to that area and bring a message of hope for the future. Among some other assignments I was specifically asked to teach a seminar on the very subject you are reading about in this book. A cold and bleak January added to the oppressive atmosphere of the city. When we arrived, we immediately felt the discouragement of the people. So many had seen their homes and livelihoods swept away by the floods. The people were devastated.

The day of my seminar came, and men and women began to file into the convention center. My notes were ready, and I was in the process of getting connected up to the microphone. For some reason I looked toward the entrance and noticed a man standing near the doorway weeping. I laid the microphone down on the table, walked over to him, and put my hand on his shoulder. With tears rolling down his cheeks, he began to tell me just how devastated he was as a result of the flood. He had lost almost everything.

Then I told him to do something strange. "My friend, I want to suggest that you do not come to my seminar." He looked at me in disbelief. Was I out of my mind, he must have thought. Here is a seminar on "Overcoming Discouragement," and the teacher tells him not to come!

"What I suggest is that you walk out of this convention building and find someone to witness to!" He looked at me in total shock and told me he had never done anything like that before. He went on to explain that he did not know what to say.

I asked him if he was a Christian, and he quickly replied he was indeed. I told him the absolute worst thing that could happen to him is that the person he witnessed to would pull out a gun and shoot him dead. In disbelief he saw me smile and tell him that the worst thing that could happen at that point was that he would go to heaven to be with the Lord, which was probably a "whole lot better than living in Grand Forks with nothing but devastation and discouragement!" I suggested he did not need to know what to say. "Simply share your testimony and let God take over." I told him that I believed in "jugular-vein evangelism," which meant the best thing to do was simply to walk up to someone and ask them if they would like to give their hearts to Jesus. After all He is the only one who can save a person. Our job is to share and leave the results up to the Lord! I watched him leave the room in fear and trepidation.

Just before I completed the one-hour seminar, I noticed him standing at the back of the room. This time he had a smile on his face. I could not wait to hear his story.

He told me he walked out to the foyer of the hotel feeling like he was going to fall apart when he noticed a well-dressed man standing against the wall with a briefcase in his hand. After swallowing a couple of times, he approached the stranger and asked, "Would you like to give your heart to the Lord Jesus?

The stranger looked at him and said, "How did you know?"

"Know what?" my new friend responded with a look of pending doom on his face.

The stranger told him that he was from Minneapolis and that his life had fallen apart. He had misappropriated funds, had lost his business and reputation, and had decided the only way out was to take his own life. He had made arrangements for his wife and kids to be taken care of and was on his way to Winnipeg, Manitoba, to end it all. Right there and then he asked the Lord Jesus Christ to come into his life!

Standing there in the entrance to that seminar room was a real eye-opening revelation to me. I looked into the face of a man who had, just minutes before, been devastated. Now he was smiling from ear to ear!

I tell you the truth. This works every time! Soul winning does not solve all problems. It does not provide much needed money. It does not, in and of itself, heal a crumbling marriage. But it does lift you out of the pit of despair. I wish more people would simply understand this as one of God's golden rules for living. It's like being nice and sweet to your wife. It always happens this way. It's a golden rule of marriage. If you leave home for work in the morning and you have behaved in an ugly manner toward your spouse, your day is going to be clouded. Whatever you do and wherever you go, there will be a fog hanging over you. But when the effort is made to be civil and loving, even if you do not feel like it, your heart will be set free.

So are you struggling to have hope and a future? Become a soul winner. Tell someone about the Lord Jesus. Be radical if necessary. Step outside the box of your own comfort zone. Use jugular-vein evangelism. Don't beat around the bush. Go for it! Lay it down the line. The worst thing that could ever happen to you is that your life will be taken. And then . . . ? What an occasion to smile and celebrate.

Chapter Seven

Stir Up the Gifts God Has Placed in You

This is perhaps the most difficult of the practical solutions to discouragement. So let me begin with a straight down-the-line statement. God's Word tells us that a failure to stir up the essential blessings and gifts God has given us will result in a life of fear and timidity. Notice what the apostle Paul had to say to Timothy, his son in the ministry:

> Therefore, I remind you to keep ablaze the gift
> of God that is in you through the laying on of
> my hands. For God has not given us a spirit
> of fearfulness, but one of power, love, and
> sound judgment. (2 Tim. 1:6–7)

Here we find the young man about to embark on the assignment the Lord had given him. Paul writes this, I believe, because God wanted Timothy and us to know something absolutely critical to life and ministry. The issue of "stirring up" carries with it the idea of continual cultivation of something special.

What is special in your life? Did you know that you were made uniquely by God with specific purposes to fulfill—all for His glory? I believe the Lord gives every Christian specific tasks and assignments. These assignments are varied and require different gifts to suit each and every person accordingly. My purpose in this book is not to help in the discovery of spiritual giftedness, but I would encourage you to make this a matter of serious business. There are many programs and ministries that can help you in this regard.

What Paul was saying to Timothy was direct and straightforward: "Take care of the cultivation of your gifts or pay the price!" In other words, he was warning Timothy that a failure to take care of the special things God had given to him would result in a sentence worse than death. Yes, that's right. To be sentenced to a life of fear and timidity is awful. Have you ever met people who may look good and may seem to have it all but are weak and ineffective in everything they do? I have. I have met grown men who have it all, so to speak, and yet they are impotent in the spiritual arena. They have little meaningful influence and "wimp out" as husbands and fathers. They have been sentenced to a life of timidity! This kind of fear is the worst kind imaginable. It renders the victim weak in action and useless in expression. I am sad to say I have met pastors like this. And what a disaster this can be. A weak and timid pastor is ineffective because it takes a man with a real sense of purpose and mission to lead a local church with effectiveness. Otherwise the ungodly will walk all over you! This is one reason there are so many fighting churches. No leadership! No one is prepared to take a stand and be counted for the Lord Jesus Christ.

I know of a dear friend who heard that some of the men in his church were "plotting" to oust the pastor at a church meeting. He gathered himself together and paid a visit to the ring leader. Without beating about the bush, he challenged him straight up and warned him not to touch the Lord's anointed. He told him that he would not stand by and allow such behavior to take place in the house of God. Today the church is thriving.

I firmly believe a person who fails to stir up and cultivate the gift God has given will, inevitably, be an unhappy person. I have yet to meet someone who is not realizing his or her full potential who is happy, fulfilled, and content. On the contrary, most people like this gradually fall into a dark hole. It is a slippery slope into the pit of despair. Here's what happens:

1. They cruise by ignoring the need to act.
2. They snooze by going to sleep on the job.
3. They refuse to accept counsel and advice.
4. They lose because they did nothing to help themselves.

Sounds a little comical, does it not? But it is true. When your disciplines fail and continual cultivation of the blessings God has given begin to be neglected, the first thing that happens is "cruise control." Sometimes months and even years can pass by without much being noticed or any outward damage taking place. The person then goes to sleep. A proverbial yawn becomes the expression of the day. Such a one develops a ho-hum kind of attitude that really couldn't care less about what anyone would have to say about it. Lethargy creeps in. It happens in marriages all the time. If disciplines are not kept in place and constantly stirred up, lethargy and laziness can quickly take hold. This is when a spouse simply quits working on that marriage and adopts the attitude of "that's just the way I am." This is a dangerous place to be. Many married men get up in the morning, slug down a cup on the way out the door, come dragging in after work, slugs down some dinner with little or no conversation, pick up the newspaper, and head for the recliner in front of the television set. Sometime later they drag themselves up to bed; and, just moments before lapsing into a state of unconsciousness, they get real upset because their wives have already gone to sleep or claim to be fighting that monstrous headache again. Hello! Going to sleep when you are in dire need of help can be disastrous.

What usually happens at this point is flat-out refusal. Most people at this stage find themselves in such a rut they are not only disinterested in help of any kind, but they refuse whatever help comes their way.

They lose! And so does everyone else who could have been blessed by this person's life.

Did you take note of what God had determined? He has not given us a spirit of fear. This is not God's plan for you and me. Note, rather, the three things He has granted to those who love Him—power, love, and a sound mind! What a triple treat! Is there anyone out there who would not want to have the blessing of these three gifts?

The basic understanding presented here lies in the fact that there are things we can do to help ourselves climb out of the fog. Many people are not simply in a bind when it comes to hope and a future. They are in a rut and can't seem to shake it. My contention supports the fact that something can be done. Based on God's Word, we can establish a foundation upon which to stand firm and upright. We can apply these principles in a practical way in our lives.

In the next section we will learn to make the resolutions that will serve to house our actions.

Part 3

Make Necessary Resolutions

Chapter One

I Am Going to Understand
Who the Enemy Is

Remember what Peter warns us about the enemy?

> Be self-controlled and alert. Your enemy the
> devil prowls around like a roaring lion looking
> for someone to devour. Resist him, standing
> firm in the faith, because you know that your
> brothers throughout the world are undergoing
> the same kind of sufferings. (1 Pet. 5:8–9 NIV)

This word of exhortation and encouragement makes
a lot of sense to me because of my upbringing in Africa.
Lions are big and powerful. Even though they are extremely
dangerous, millions of tourists line up to watch them and

"ooh" and "ah" as they take photos. Baby lions are particularly enticing because they look so cute and cuddly. But even though something may look inviting, it can be deadly. Satan is a master tactician who, just like the lion, prowls around looking for his victim without discrimination. His hunger pangs do not discriminate based on gender, social standing, or anything else for that matter. When he wants to eat, he goes out to eat!

The Bible's lessons about our enemy are not to be relegated to a dusty shelf. They are timeless truths. God wrote it all down for you and me because He wants us always to understand and resist the tactics of this monster. He loves us so much He wants us to be prepared for the onslaught and, when it comes, to stand up straight and face our roaring lions head-on.

Chapter Two

I Am Going to Recognize Satan's Tactics

Ten Tactics of Satan

1. Satan causes doubt. From the very beginning we find Satan making every effort to impugn, or point the finger at the character of God.

> Now the serpent was more crafty than any of
> the wild animals the LORD God had made. He
> said to the woman, "Did God really say, 'You
> must not eat from any tree in the garden'?" The
> woman said to the serpent, "We may eat fruit
> from the trees in the garden, but God did say,
> 'You must not eat fruit from the tree that is in

the middle of the garden, and you must not
touch it, or you will die." "You will not surely
die," the serpent said to the women. "For God
knows that when you eat of it your eyes will
be opened, and you will be like God, knowing
good and evil. (Gen. 3:1–5 NIV)

Jesus had harsh words for some of the Jews who opposed
Him during His earthly ministry: "You belong to your
father, the devil, and you want to carry out your father's
desire. He was a murderer from the beginning, not holding
to the truth, for there is no truth in him. When he lies, he
speaks his native language, for he is a liar and the father of
lies" (John 8:44 NIV).

Satan tries to discredit God in our lives, and we must be
careful not to believe the lies of the evil one.

2. Satan deceives. The evil one does everything he can
to rob people of their joy in life. He instigates persecution,
enlists people to carry out his devious schemes, promotes
family feuds, spreads gossip, and starts rumors. All of this
accounts for a difficult journey and an arduous, or tough,
Christian walk that demands a bold and determined faith
and trust in God.

3. Satan distorts truth. In his letter to the Christians
at Ephesus, Paul reminds God's standard bearers of their
essential duty to prepare God's people for works of service
and to strive toward the goal of unity among God's people. The reason, Paul stresses, is so that "we will no longer
be infants, tossed back and forth by the waves, and blown

here and there by every wind of teaching and by the cunning and craftiness of men in their deceitful scheming" (Eph. 4:14 NIV).

Satan is the arch deceiver. He is a master of his craft and has only one desire, and that is to destroy you and rob you of any hope and any future. His favorite thing to do is to pounce on you with a sneak attack.

It reminds me of the scourge of gambling. Just one drive down Interstate 10 on the gulf coast of Mississippi will leave you in no doubt as to the meaning of a sneak attack. Each billboard, one after the other, paints a deceitful picture. From Mobile, Alabama, to Pascagoula, from Biloxi to the John Stennis Space Center, Satan displays his enticing thumbprint. It all looks so good. "Come to us," they say. "Bring your money and have a good time." "The food is outstanding and cheap, and the returns are unbelievable!" And just think about all the little boys and girls who will benefit because of the money given to education! Now who can argue with the education of our children?

What is not displayed on these billboards are the bankrupt people, destroyed marriages, and broken lives. They don't tell you about all the poor people who cash their meager earnings in the hope of a future that seldom materializes. They spotlight one or two "lucky" individuals who are used as examples of just how lucky you could be if you were willing to forgo your check as well. All it takes is just one roll of the dice. All it takes is just one pull of the lever and you have it made!

4. Satan distracts attention. As Paul went about his ministry, he lamented the fact that he would have to stay on at Ephesus "because a great door for effective work has opened to me, and there are many who oppose me" (1 Cor. 16:8–9 NIV). Later on the apostle even refers to his "thorn in the flesh." He suggests who was responsible for giving this "thorn" to him and why God allowed it to be given to him:

> To keep me from becoming conceited because
> of these surpassingly great revelations, there
> was given me a thorn in my flesh, a messenger
> of Satan, to torment me. Three times I pleaded
> with the Lord to take it away from me. But
> he said to me, "My grace is sufficient for you,
> for my power is made perfect in weakness."
> Therefore I will boast all the more gladly about
> my weaknesses, so that Christ's power may rest
> on me. That is why, for Christ's sake,
> I delight in weakness, in insults, in hardships,
> in persecutions, in difficulties. For when I am
> weak, then I am strong. (2 Cor. 12:7–10 NIV)

This servant of the Lord was confronted with one satanic distraction after another. Yet he stayed the course and overcame his discouragement. He knew where his hope and future lay.

Satan will also use circumstances and the lure of pleasure to divert your attention. It really is amazing how he does this. Take the matter of physical wellness. In my own life this is a real challenge. I have had numerous times in my life when, by God's grace alone, I have been able to discipline myself to eat properly and exercise regularly. One thing I do know for certain is that I feel a whole lot better when I do. My mind is sharper, and I don't feel as though I am a beached whale. The bottom line when it comes to my weight and wellness is that my entire life just works better when I am in good shape physically. I really believe I am able to serve the Lord Jesus in a much more effective manner when I am in control of my body. I sleep better, enjoy food better, and even threaten my family that I may put on a Speedo and walk down the beach!

Perhaps the greatest blessing lies in my passion to serve my Savior and Lord. When I get out of shape, it hurts my testimony. Nobody says anything, and I know they love me just as I am, but it is not a good witness. I am also far more productive in my study habits. I need heaps of energy, and I certainly do not need to get down and become depressed.

But when I let go of my own physical well-being, it happens. It makes me feel awful, and sometimes I really have to put on a game face to get through the day. And it always starts with diversions and distractions. I believe that old scheming snake gets me to think that I am immortal. He convinces me I really don't need to go to the fitness center. Before long, my one day missed here and another skipped there rolls into months. One little extra plate of fries quickly becomes the consumption of a fried potato farm.

The enemy goes to great lengths to divert our attention so he can make us conform to his devious ways.

5. *Satan promotes divisions.* Christians are urged to "make every effort to keep the unity of the Spirit through the bond of peace" (Eph. 4:3 NIV). This urging comes in light of Satan's tactic to promote division among God's people. Paul calls this "the desires of the sinful nature" (Gal. 5:16 NIV) and leaves no doubt that those factions and divisions find their root source in the heart of Satan.

The devil uses deceitful leaders to divide the church. Jude reports, "For certain men whose condemnation was written about long ago have secretly slipped in among you. They are godless men, who change the grace of our God into a license for immorality and deny Jesus Christ our only Sovereign and Lord" (Jude 4 NIV).

The Lord Jesus gives this warning:

> Watch out for false prophets. They come to
> you in sheep's clothing, but inwardly they are
> ferocious wolves. By their fruit you will recognize
> them. Do people pick grapes from thornbushes,
> or figs from thistles? Likewise every good tree
> bears good fruit, but a bad tree bears bad fruit.
> A good tree cannot bear bad fruit, and a bad tree
> cannot bear good fruit. Every tree that does not
> bear good fruit is cut down and thrown into the
> fire. Thus, by their fruit you will recognize them.
> (Matt. 7:15–20 NIV)

6. Satan is determined. One thing we know about the Energizer bunny: He keeps going and going and going! But he is only a toy and occupies a very small space in a world of make-believe. Not so when it comes to the devil. He does indeed keep going and going and going, but he is not a toy. He is not make-believe. The devil and his demons occupy the real world.

The enemy does not let go easily. He persists in a relentless pursuit to bring his victim down. Remember the roaring lion. Such animals are well known for the relentless persistence with which they both stalk and attack their prey. They scope out the territory in fine detail. They mark selected spots so as to ensure other predators do not venture too close to them, and they exercise great patience because they have the end in mind.

The victims, for the most part, consider themselves to be safe and secure, especially when in the herd. The company they keep provides not only companionship but also security, or so they think. Many video recordings bear testimony to the ferocious charge and battle cry of a roaring lion as it pounces on the herd. Dust flies, hooves thump, and panic breaks out as the victims flee for their lives. Sometimes the lion misses his target. Something gets in the way, or his timing might have been off. But do not be mistaken. He will be back. And the next time he will succeed.

Now observe the rest of the herd. Judging by the look on their faces, one might detect a small glimmer of sadness and despair at the demise of their former companion. A mother may turn around and come back just in case there may be one slight glimmer of hope for the survival of her offspring. But it does not take long before they all get on with their lives.

How quickly people move on! But Satan does not forget, and he does not move on. He persists with a relentless determination to get you where he wants you to be. Down-and-out with no hope and certainly no future!

7. Satan drops hints. This has been covered sufficiently in my previous discussion, but I must sound the alarm again. Satan is a slippery snake who slithers his slimy way into marriages, homes, relationships, and every circumstance imaginable. He is like a bad breath sitting on the shoulder of all who give occasion to whisper in their ears.

8. Satan disguises his evil ways. As we have already noted, even the Lord Jesus warned us that "wolves in sheep's clothing" would assault some. Satan, after all, is the master masquerader and the lord of disguise.

9. Satan devours people. This "roaring lion" prowls around the empty streets at night, slithers around the hallways of our schools, and infiltrates every home and heart that provides him room to breathe. He has but one goal in mind: to devour people. This is what the Lord Jesus had to say about him: "The thief comes only to steal and kill and destroy" (John 10:10 NIV).

10. Satan dispatches demons. Satan is in charge of all the forces of evil, including his legions of demons. They stand ready to do his bidding and jump into action at his command. They represent their terrible commander and inhabit the lives of people. Jesus encountered many who were demon possessed. In one such encounter Jesus gave the demons permission to enter a large herd of pigs feeding on a hillside. When they came out of the man, they went into the pigs, and the herd rushed down the steep bank into the lake and was drowned (Luke 8:26–39).

Satan uses these ten tactics to infiltrate, maim, kill, and destroy. He is at work and will do whatever it takes to take you down. Be informed, be aware, be warned, be prepared, and be encouraged "because the One who is in you is greater than the one who is in the world" (1 John 4:4). Always claim the promise that you can do it with God's help. You can claim the victory and triumph over your circumstances. You can conquer the demons that confront you. Remember the conditional promise of God's Word that if you resist the devil, "he will flee from you" (James 4:7).

Why Does God Allow These Things to Happen?

If God loves me and protects me, then why does He allow Satan to go to work on me? I think there are three plausible responses to this age-old question:

1. Purification. God wants me to be pure. Perhaps He allows these things to happen in order to make me pure. Our lives are so filled with junk that we become clogged up.

When we are challenged through life's circumstances and we remain faithful, obedient, and dependent on God, we can become pure in heart. We are made like new again.

2. Burning. Like the master goldsmith who burns away the dross and impurities until he can see his own reflection in the gold, so it is that our heavenly Father allows us to be refined by fire so as to see His reflection in our lives.

This would certainly be true in my own life. When I first came to the wonderful church I now serve, I went through a pretty tough time. I would be less than honest if I did not readily admit to many nights of deep anguish and pain. It is never easy to see people behave badly, and it is never easy to watch people walk out of your church, no matter what the reason. During those early years both my wife and I spent quite a few days wondering if we had really followed the Lord's leadership in accepting the call to pastor the church or simply followed a dream. Satan really went to work, and he undoubtedly raised up his Sanballat, Tobiah, and quite a few Arabs and Ammonites with them. They stood out like sore thumbs in the middle of a wonderful group of godly people. But it was tough going for a while. There were rumors and suggestions, and of course, Sanballat and his entourage would show up at business meetings in full force. He used all kinds of tactics to spread his foul breath through the house of God. One day a godly man told me, "Never get into a pigpen with a hog. You will both get covered in mud, and the pig will love it!"

Great advice for a man being driven into the pits of depression. I made the decision to try my best never to get into the pigpen and to some extent succeeded. But as I look back from the vantage point of so much joy, I now realize the Lord allowed all this to happen with one man in mind. All the junk (or at least a lot of it) needed to be burned out of my life. God wanted me to be the man of God He intended me to be, and evidently I had (and still have) a long way to go.

3. Identification. This is the third reason God allows us to go through deep waters. Some people take a lifetime to realize that the onslaught of Satan is real. A number of older people have remarked that they wished they had learned earlier in life about the reality of the evil one. Perhaps the Lord is just being too kind to you. Without ever suggesting that your pain is something to celebrate, I am suggesting you may be blessed in a way you may not fully realize.

My middle son, Greg, had a fender bender shortly after he became eligible to drive at the tender age of fifteen. I remember the call that came from down the road to say that he had been in an accident. Anxiously his mother and I jumped into the car and drove to the scene. Much to our relief someone had run a traffic light and had only dented his front bumper. In a way we were grateful for the wreck because it taught him a lesson at an early stage of his life. Besides, he was unhurt. I think it slowed him down—at least for a while!

Does God allow these things to happen? Just think about Job! Perhaps it is necessary for us to go through deep waters so that we can identify our adversary. It is similar to the many forms of cancer. From prostate cancer to breast cancer, we are told that early detection is the key. This is why it is so important to get checked out, no matter how uncomfortable it may be! When the beginnings of cancer are detected, the chances of survival are far greater.

What Can We Do about It?

Without making an effort either to repeat myself or to get ahead of what I am going to say, I think it is important to suggest the following things you can do right now in response to the attacks you are being faced with:

- Be prayerful. Don't stop seeking God's face in prayer.
- Be alert. Don't ignore your situation.
- Be decisive. Take all necessary steps God puts before you.
- Be thankful. Remember that Paul has taught us to be thankful and content no matter what our circumstances.

I remember hearing my friend Dr. Billy Graham saying, "Your future is as bright as the promises of God!"

Chapter Three

I Am Resisting the Enemy

Once we understand the tactics he uses to get to us, we can turn our attention to the kind of weaponry God has made available for us to fight the enemy.

Finally, be strong in the Lord and in his mighty power. Put on the full armor of God so that you can take your stand against the devil's schemes. For our struggle is not against flesh and blood, but against the rulers, against the authorities, against the powers of this dark world and against the spiritual forces of evil in the heavenly realms. Therefore put on the full armor of God, so that when the day of evil comes, you may be able to stand your ground,

and after you have done everything, to stand.
Stand firm then, with the belt of truth buckled
around your waist, with the breastplate of
righteousness in place, and with your feet fitted
with the readiness that comes from the gospel
of peace. In addition to all this, take up the
shield of faith, with which you can extinguish
all the flaming arrows of the evil one. Take the
helmet of salvation and the sword of the Spirit,
which is the word of God. And pray in the
Spirit on all occasions with all kinds of prayers
and requests. With this in mind, be alert and
always keep on praying for all the saints.
(Eph. 6:10–18 NIV)

Once again we can conclude with the authority of God's
Word that Satan is not only alive and real, but he is extremely
active and readily engaged in the affairs of people. More
specifically, he is actively engaged in the lives of Christian
people. He wants a piece of us, and he is determined to get
us where he wants us to be—down and out, depressed and
discouraged!

This wonderful passage carries seven golden rules of
engagement or commitment. Each one describes a decisive action to be taken in light of the attacks we face. These
seven golden rules of engagement lie at the heart of hope
and are essential in the guarantee of a bright and meaningful future.

The Seven Golden Rules of Engagement

1. Be strong (v. 10). This mandate carries the idea that our faith must be engaged to the fullest extent. We often read in the newspaper of someone who is being prosecuted to the fullest extent of the law. This means that no limits will be placed on the prosecution in terms of the pursuit of justice. When Paul provided the foundation for spiritual leadership in what is known as the Pastoral Epistles, he was sure to underscore just how important it is to be bold in the exercise of our faith. The first golden rule is a pillar of strength to stand on. It is the foundation of our action. Paul is saying that we must depend on who we know, and we must depend on what we know about who we know. Be strong in Christ Jesus because He is the one who is able to do exceedingly abundantly more than we could ever imagine we are capable of doing. Bottom line—trust God!

2. Put on (v. 11). Every morning when I wake up I put on my clothes. And so it is with this second golden rule. The expression here is forceful and dynamic. This is not a suggestion for some of us to take into consideration when and if we feel like it. So many believers actually think God sets before them a series of options for them to consider. This is not an option. "You must 'put on'," Paul is demanding because this is the only means by which you are going to stand strong and have a hope and a future. Furthermore, the implication here is not for a partial covering but rather a complete covering. Note the emphasis on what we need to put on. "The full armor of God" is exactly what it says it is—the full armor! Many Christians just don't get it! A half-dressed Christian is a walking target for the evil one because so many gaps are left in his or her defense system. We are instructed to be strong in our faith, and we are told to get dressed properly and completely as we journey through the difficulties of life.

3. Take your stand (v. 11b). Once having been instructed to "put on" the full covering of all God has made available to us, we are now instructed to spring into action. This means, "Get going." I have always loved the accounts of the famous British cavalry Light Brigade because they epitomized decisive action. The movie depiction of the famous scene shows this army of gallant soldiers, dressed to the hilt with swords drawn and charging toward the enemy. They knew the odds were against them, but they had three things on their side. They were "strong" in their belief in themselves, they had "put on" all the weaponry needed for an epic battle, and they were "taking up" the mantle of their responsibility and charging into action. In these verses God is both reminding us to spring into action while at the same time warning us not to be passive. The Christian life is not an armchair experience. If you simply sit down and wait for the devil to bring it on, you will be crushed. He is a powerful adversary! He will not mess around with you and is by no means Mr. Nice Guy. Once you have reaffirmed your faith and trust in God's all-powerful ability, and once you have fully awakened and dressed yourself in God's complete outfit, it is time to take it to the devil.

4. Stand firm (v. 14). The fourth rule of engagement is a tough one. It reminds me of one of my fondest memories growing up on the shores of the magnificent Indian Ocean. Scattered along the spectacular Natal and Cape shoreline are the most fantastic beaches in the world. The rocks, gullies, shells, and crashing blue sea will always have a special place in my heart and memory. Among the many marks of distinction are the tidal swimming pools. These tidal pools are literally hewn out of the natural rock that is a part of the coastal landscape. With a few constructive additions and adjustments, these swimming pools jut out into the sea so that the full force of the crashing waves is the only means by which they are filled with water. Needless to say, these are saltwater pools. As children we used to love venturing out to the outer wall of these pools. I can picture my brothers and me daring one another to stand up on those walls and wait for a wave to come crashing over the edge and into the pool. And what fun! We would stand up with our hearts pumping in our chests, brace ourselves, and wait for the inevitable "thump," "whoosh," and force of the crashing wave as it built up and then crashed into the wall, up and over and into the pool. With much yelling and screaming from those in the pool, the "victim" would be totally engulfed by the wave. We would hold our breath, waiting for the waves to subside and to see if the victim had been strong enough to stand his or her ground.

This is the picture given here with this fourth golden rule of engagement. "Stand firm then" carries such a charge to plant your feet firmly in the ground with your head held up high and face the onslaught of the enemy with a renewed determination and fresh confidence that God will not let you down!

5. *Take up the Shield (v. 16)*. This wonderful fifth golden rule of engagement is where "the water hits the wheel." It certainly is the most challenging part because it takes place during the actual onslaught.

Many years ago my brother, Rod, took his daughters Christy and Hayley on a ski trip in the mountains of North Carolina. My understanding is that he was skiing down a track when he heard some people yelling and pointing up at the passing ski lift. There he saw his two daughters. Christy was firmly in the lift chair with her skis on, but Hayley had slipped and was literally dangling for life. Her sister was holding on to her jacket to keep her from falling while Hayley was desperately holding on to one of the bars on the ski lift itself. By God's grace they made it to the point where they could unload at the top of the hill. It still causes a heart palpitation in me just to think about how easily we could have lost Hayley to this accident.

This is what we are told to do at this point. But note the sequence of instruction again. The first thing to do is to "be strong" in the Lord. Then we are to get fully dressed as we "put on" the whole uniform of God's armor. Next it is time to "stand firm" and spring into action. The action begins, and we are now told to "hold on." In other words, don't give up regardless of where you are in the battle.

6. Pray in the Spirit (v. 18). Verse 18 is pivotal when it comes to having a hope and a future. "And pray in the Spirit on all occasions with all kinds of prayers and requests." Prayer is the key ingredient. It is the heart of our action and the soul of our dependency. Without prayer we are rendered useless. Without prayer we are declared powerless. God invites us to seek His face continually and constantly, no matter what our circumstances. We must bow down in His presence! This means there are no exceptions to the rule. God does not make Himself available to us at some times and not at others. This does not mean He is available to give us an immediate answer. Sometimes the Lord needs for us to wait on Him simply because those who "wait upon the LORD shall renew their strength" (Isa. 40:31 KJV). At other times He will give us what seems to be a partial answer, perhaps because He wants us to think through our circumstances before we take any action. The issue here is not the response we receive but rather the fact we are engaged in a conversation with the only one who is capable of rendering a verdict.

7. Be Alert (v. 18b). This is the final golden rule of engagement and must be seriously taken into consideration before we determine how this armor works in God's economy. I think the most direct imperative is this one. "With this in mind, be alert." Wow! Watch out and be continually careful, Paul is saying. Don't let your guard down. Not even for a second. The roaring lion is out there, and he is on the prowl. He has your number, and he is hungry. Nothing in his mind can stop him, excepting the King of kings and the Lord of lords. Satan knows who God is. He believes in Him. He knows he is doomed, but there is nothing he loves more than a Christian who is "wishy-washy" in his or her faith and determination. Nothing pleases Satan more than to find a weak Christian who thinks he can go it alone. Nothing makes him happier than to watch the divisions and jealousies and anger and lack of commitment on the part of so many of us.

Be alert, Paul pleads with a cry from his heart and a dogged determination to get it into our stubborn heads that the Lord Jesus loves us. He is Lord and always has been Lord. He has never changed, and His love for us has never changed. His demands are just the same as they have always been.

We are to deny ourselves to the point at which everything we hold dear looses its relevance. We are to attach ourselves to the finished work of the Lord Jesus Christ on the cross to the point at which we become fused and amalgamated into His life. This is why Paul stated that for him to live was Christ and to die was total gain. Why? Because his life and the life of Christ Jesus were inseparable. This is why we need to be alert. This alertness reminds us continually of our inseparable attachment to the Lord Jesus Christ.

I remember the great story of the 1992 Olympics runner, Derek Redmond, who had trained so hard and for so long to have his moment in the spotlight and run for his country. He had spent years in preparation and had arrived at the track fully equipped and prepared to run the race of his life. It was not to be, however, as he suddenly came up short with a race-ending injury that left him weeping in pain as the whole world watched his agony. Then, when all seemed lost, a man emerged at his side. With compassion this other man lifted the runner up and began to assist him across the finish line. History records the deafening roar of the crowds cheering for this dad who had come from out of the grandstand to carry his son across the line.

This is how we see the Lord Jesus. He loves us so much. He will carry us through every trial and every circumstance of life because He is our hope and our future!

Chapter Four

I Am Going to Get Properly Dressed

This is the part where we have to knuckle down and actually do some practical things as we apply God's Word in our lives. I am always reminded of King David and his troubles, all of which were the result of his own sin and disobedience. This man committed adultery with Bathsheba, killed her husband, and then flat-out lied to God's servant about the whole scenario. When he came to his senses, God certainly forgave him and restored the "joy of his salvation" to him—but not without practical application. As much as we are taught to "think on these things," we are also taught to do these things.

The same can be said of the prodigal son. Jesus told us about this young man who went to his father and asked that he be given his inheritance so he could go and spend it any way he wanted to spend it. Off he went to a faraway country where he squandered his inheritance in sinful and riotous living. Things got so bad he lost it all and ended up in the pigsty, eating the garbage that was given to the pigs to eat. Right there in the middle the muck and mud he came to his senses and realized that his father's house provided all he would ever need in life. Even his father's hired hands and servants were treated better than he was. So he got up and went back to his father's house. While he was still a long way off, he saw his father running out of his home with his arms open wide in an embrace of love, forgiveness, and acceptance. But he had to get up and get dressed for the occasion. Nothing much would have happened if he had simply thought about the possibilities.

And so it is when it comes to our situation and circumstances. Some of us are simply under attack from the enemy because he knows we are prime targets. If he can get to us and break us down and destroy our hope and our future, he has a real feather in his cap. He thinks he has scored a huge knockout blow against God Jehovah, the one he hates with such venom and passion. On the other hand, many of us are in the pigpens of life because we have allowed sin to reign in our mortal bodies. Sin has captivated us and has captured our hearts. We have given way and have given in and are suffering the consequences. You know which of these two scenarios you are in, and you know what you have done and have not done.

Getting dressed properly applies whether sin has been the cause of our distress or whether we feel we are simply under attack from the enemy.

Paul's injunction to the Ephesian believers carries two directives related to the armor of God. First, God wants us to wear permanent protection. Second, God invites us to wear available protection.

God Wants Us to Wear Permanent Protection

As we dress according to the Lord's instructions, it is important to note that the first three articles of armor are not only designed for long-range protection, but they are also designed for long-term protection. These articles of armor are the belt, the breastplate, and the shoes. This is how we are to do it based on Ephesians 6:

1. By buckling up (v. 14). One thing I do know is this: when I buckle up my trousers in the morning it certainly prevents unnecessary exposure! It also helps greatly to give me confidence for the day, while, at the same time, my belt enables me to be presented to the world in a decent way. The belt of God's truth does three things for us.

It is the content of what is true. God literally invites us to strap His Word around our waists as we face each and every day. This will mean we have God's promises harnessed about us continually and constantly. The Word of God acts as an instant resource in at least two ways. It prevents us from falling into sin and provokes us into action. When we hide God's Word in (around) our hearts, we are inoculated with the only antidote strong enough to withstand the onslaught of Satan. At the same time we are also given the only solid means by which we can throw God back at Satan when he attacks. Satan regards us as powder puffs when we try to stand against him in and of ourselves. But when he has to tackle the Lord Jesus Christ, he knows he has been defeated even before he has begun.

It is the attitude of what is true. As I write this book, there is a big debate going on about baggy pants! Some young people look like they are wearing pants, but they have nothing to hold them up. Right or wrong, the arguments revolve around the obvious subject of decency, but they also revolve around the matter of attitude. I believe the belt of God's eternal truth bears testimony to an attitude. This kind of attitude is not proud, arrogant, or rude in any way. Rather, the belt of God's truth is a reminder to the wearer that he is held together by something far greater than himself. It is also a reminder to the foes out there that they are dealing with someone who has an attitude that rests squarely on the mind of Christ. Implied in this is a spiritual threat, in a way. There is a sense in which the wearer of this belt is stepping into the ring in a world heavyweight-boxing bout. The only difference between the wearer of the belt and his opponent is that he has the championship already. The challenger is trying to get it away from him. This is exactly who Satan fancies himself to be. He thinks he is about to become the world heavyweight champion, but when he sees that belt around his opponent, he knows he doesn't stand a chance!

It is the commitment of what is true. God's belt of truth also gives courage to the wearer as he or she contemplates the future. One of the greatest struggles we have, especially when faced with depression and discouragement, is the future. It is hard enough to think clearly in the present, let alone in the future. The wonderful thing about the Word of God is that it's timelessness. Everything about our Savior is eternal. He knows about me today and has every detail of my life firmly in the palm of His hand for tomorrow.

So why did the Lord choose a belt for part of His armor? Back in Paul's day the Romans wore a sort of dress-looking thing, if you will beg my pardon. I certainly am glad I don't have to wear one of those things today! Nonetheless, these Roman garments had to be harnessed together or gathered up for three important reasons. First, they were gathered up with a belt in order to demonstrate readiness. Without the belt, they looked rather sloppy and untidy. It gave the wrong impression to others and especially to their opponents. Second, they were gathered up to prevent clumsiness. An unkempt person looks clumsy and disheveled. Sometimes even appearances can provide an open door for problems. I remember suggesting to a man that he "clean himself up" when he and his wife came to see me about some problems they were having. If I were a woman, I would not have wanted to be married to him. He looked like he had been dragged through a bush backwards. His hair was all over the place; his fingernails were flat-out disgusting. They were so filthy I did not want to look at them. He was grossly overweight, to say the least, and he seemed to have serious bad breath every time he spoke to me.

The belt of truth will enable you to get rid of an unkempt Christian life! This belt prevents any thought of clumsiness and disorder. But, third, the Roman belt also eliminated any encumbrances. I could not even imagine trying to run with one of those things on. But that was the way they dressed. I recently read a good biography of Cicero, the great orator, senator, and statesman in the decades leading up to the birth of the Lord Jesus Christ in Bethlehem. What intrigued me so much was the chaos of Rome. Nobody was safe and everybody wanted a piece of everybody. The murders, battles, immorality, and terror of that day were something else. No wonder the Lord Jesus had to deal with the likes of Caesar Augustus and Pontius Pilate. The point is that Paul was relating the vital importance of a belt to show us that life without it could be deadly. Without the Word of truth securely buckled around your waist, you are left entirely to your own encumbrances!

2. By strapping on (v. 14b). The breastplate of righteousness was an interesting piece of armor. It had to be practically strapped on the front of the body and usually required some help from another person. Regiments of Roman soldiers organized themselves in such a way that they could literally assist one another with these vital pieces of equipment. This is why friends, pastors, teachers, and so many others are always available to help us in our preparation for the battle around us. We all help one another. But this is no ordinary breastplate. Paul calls it the breastplate of righteousness. Perhaps he had in mind the fruit of God's imputed righteousness. God's imputed righteousness is what God does for us in and through the Lord Jesus. When I give my life to Christ, God confers His own righteousness on me because of the sacrifice of the Lord Jesus Christ. This is why Christ lives in me. Even though I am living this life, Christ takes up residence in me by His Spirit. This is not something you and I can do for us. It is all God and no man! But the breastplate of God's righteousness is the outward covering given to man representing the inward coating of God's grace in his heart and life. The breastplate is placed in my hands, and I must strap it on myself, taking what the Lord has made available to me and placing it over my heart and life. In modern-day terminology the breastplate becomes the feet of my faith. It is the applied theology of my understanding of who I am in Christ. Far too many people trust Jesus as their Savior and Lord and then believe they have nothing to do themselves. Being a Christian involves jolly hard work. The call to Christian discipleship means following in the footsteps of the Master. It has feet. This imperative to strap on the breastplate of righteousness carries with it the notion of action on the part of the soldier.

It reminds me of the story about the man on the roof of his house when the floods came. The police came in a boat, and he refused to jump in the boat. A helicopter came to pluck him from the roof, and he refused to be harnessed to safety. He drowned! The story goes that in heaven he asked why God had not saved him from drowning. God answered, "Son, I sent you a boat and a helicopter, but you refused to strap into them!"

Sounds like you and me! God's imputed righteousness is what God has done for us. It is not dependant on us in any way. But the breastplate of God's righteousness is an entirely different matter. This is what God has sent our way. He requires we take hold of it and strap it on! Below are things the breastplate does for us:

- The breastplate protects us. It covers our vital organs, especially our hearts. One shot in the heart and you are dead.
- The breastplate prevents us. It is God's insurance policy because it prevents us from being subject to surprise attacks, one of Satan's favorite things to do.
- The breastplate preserves us. It gives us daily peace and assurance in our hearts. Worry is one of the greatest thieves in the world today. Many people worry about things that have not even happened yet, and the more they worry the more stress they have, and the more stress they have the greater the battlefield of life. This breastplate of God's

righteousness holds our hearts in the palm of God's hands.

God wants us to wear permanent protection by buckling up with the belt of truth and by strapping on the breastplate of God's righteousness. Now He wants us to put on shoes.

3. By putting on (v. 15). I am a son of Africa. That is where I was born and raised. And so I guess I must admit that shoes were not always on top of my list as a youngster. But the older I am, the softer my feet have become. At a young age I developed calluses on the soles of my feet and so was able to withstand much more than I can today when I went about without shoes on my feet. The Lord is letting us know that shoes are an indispensable part of the Christian's wardrobe if we are to enjoy the peace of God. People who are in turmoil have no peace. Conflict robs us of peace, and when hope and a future take a backseat, peace flies out the door. Most people who are depressed and discouraged will tell you they have no peace. The world is looking for peace, and if there is any way Satan can destroy you, he will do so by taking away your sense of peace.

Look at this verse closely. "And with your feet fitted with the readiness that comes from the gospel of peace" (v. 15 NIV). How can shoes and peace be linked together here? Consider some of the things that can really hurt when you walk about barefoot. There are thorns everywhere and they hurt. Rocks can cut you to pieces. Sometimes the ground can be so hot it really hurts to walk without shoes. I remember sprinting across beaches in South Africa, desperate to reach the water because the soles of my feet were being burned up. Shoes can also provide much needed traction, especially when the surface is slippery and wet. The list could go on.

God wants us to put shoes on our feet so we can be totally ready to spring into action at any moment and so we can be assured of His abiding peace. It is also worth noting that these shoes are "fitted" for us. God has made designer shoes for every individual for whom He died. He doesn't have a mass plan. We serve a personal Savior who enters into a personal relationship with you and me. Someone once asked me what the difference was between his religion and my Christianity. First, I told him I am not a religious person. I am a Christian man. Most of the world is religious. Most people believe in something or someone. Even atheists are religious. In fact I believe they believe in God. They are certainly not saved because they reject Him, but they believe in Him even though they say there is no God. If they really believed there is no God, they would not spend so much time and effort trying to prove God does not exist! Why burst a blood vessel trying to prove the nonexistence of someone you do not believe exists? The second thing I told him was that I have a personal relationship with the living God. My Savior is not only real and personal, but He is alive and well!

Put on God's shoes. They will give you permanent protection and enable you to be ready at a moments' notice. But the Lord also wants us to wear available protection.

God Wants Us to Wear Available Protection

The suit of armor the Lord provides for His children is truly magnificent. While the first three articles provide permanent protection for the journey of life, the latter three are no less significant. Some may regard the shield, the helmet, and the sword as accessories, but I think not. It would be pretty tough for a soldier to go into battle without any one of these three articles. They are essential, unless, of course, God intends for us to be part of the medical corps!

Now the medical corps personnel are a vital part of any military team. Of that there is no doubt. Back in my day in the service, the members of the medical corps were totally unarmed. My tank squadron found themselves in a "hull down" position on the top of a rather steep hill. This means the tanks were positioned in such a way that, while they faced the enemy camp, their long turrets were dropped down so as not to stick out for the enemy to detect. At the same time, the gun turrets could be raised at a moment's notice and be ready to fire. As the leader of the group, I had a full-size Land Rover at my disposal. My driver drove the Rover to the bottom of the hill where the battalion commander had ordered all officers to gather for a powwow. As we gathered around him, someone suddenly yelled that my tank was slowly backing down the hill and directly toward the parked Land Rover. I dove into one door to try to get the Rover out of the way and then, realizing it was too late, scrambled out the other door just as this huge tank mounted the vehicle and gradually and painfully crushed it into the ground. We scrambled to the top of the tank, opened the hatch, and observed a frightened member of the medical corps trying desperately to become invisible at the lowest level of the tank. Evidently he had climbed up and into the tank and had tampered with the auxiliary system. The turret had slowly turned backward, transferring all the weight to the back of the tank and had somehow released the brake system resulting in the demolition of my Land Rover! This young medic knew how to tend the wounded, but he was not properly prepared for the battlefield.

Many of us go out into the world just like this young man. We are trained in many ways and certainly provide great service to many. We study the Word of God on occasion and even attend church from time to time. Some of us do wonderful acts in the name of the Lord, and when called on, we are usually available. But we are not fully dressed. We go so far but not far enough. We serve but on our terms. We give of our finances but so long as it does not hurt or affect us in any way. Churches today are filled with partially committed Christians. We do not understand, and some do not accept, that God demands equal sacrifice, not equal giving. What He wants is all of us, and He will not settle for anything less than all of us.

Scores of us fill the streets of our world. We face every kind of difficulty known to man. We suffer great loss and go through excruciating pain. We strive to please others and yet face the relentless onslaught of Satan at every turn.

We attend all the ball games of our sons and daughters, we pick up the trash after the church services, and we volunteer to drive the bus anytime we are needed. But we are insufficiently dressed for the battlefield. We are willing to go only so far and no farther.

Listen carefully to this. A partially dressed believer is a vulnerable believer. God has made available to all of us the additions we need to complement the permanent protection we must wear. So pick up your shield, pull over your helmet, and hold on to your sword because it is imperative you have them. If you do not listen and act, then you may find yourself at the lowest point of your life, trying to hide from reality while careening down a slippery slope to a pending disaster. This is what to do next. This is how God wants us to have His available protection.

1. By taking up (v. 16). This is a deliberate action! Shields do not have a habit of suddenly picking themselves up and jumping into the arms of a soldier! The shield He makes available to us is a big one. Back in Paul's day the Roman soldier's shield literally covered most of his body. It was a heavy instrument and had a number of huge crisscrossed straps on the inside designed to rope the arm through them. The idea was to thread one arm through the straps and fasten them down in such a manner that the shield would remain in a firm and locked-down position even in the heat of battle. Soldiers never had to be told to hold on to that shield. If it came loose or was pried away somehow, he knew his chances for survival were dramatically reduced. The shield was designed to do two major things:

It was designed to form a protective devise for the protector. Because it covered most of the front parts of the body, it stands to reason that this shield covered the warrior's vital organs.

The shield of faith is not only designed to cover your vital organs, but it has maneuverability. This is why it is attached to the arm. Although the shield was frightfully heavy, the rigorous training every soldier was expected to go through gave him the physical strength and power to move the shield up and down and even from side to side in quick response to any arrow or sword headed in his direction.

Faith is that shield. It is the fabric of our relationship with God in and through the Lord Jesus Christ. It is the foundation upon which we stand. It forms the crust of our conviction and provides the content of our determination. Martin Luther took his stand and precipitated the great Protestant Reformation because he came to the point at which he realized we have been declared just and righteous before a holy God by means of faith. If you do not pick up this wonderful article, you will leave yourself exposed to everyone and everything Satan throws at you. You must also learn to maneuver your faith in such a manner to prevent Satan from attacking where you least expect it. If not, you instantly become prime time in Satan's economy because so much more than just your Achilles' heel is left exposed. Your heart is laid bare for the darts of the wicked one, and your lungs become a screaming open invitation for a puncture hole. If your lungs or heart are punctured, you're dead, my friend!

It was designed to form a protective device for fellow warriors, or we might call them protectees. While you, the shield bearer, are the protector, the protectees are the ones God gives you to protect. A good example of a protector is a mother, while a good example of a protectee is her child. The same can be applied in a teacher/student relationship or a pastor/congregation relationship. There are many other examples.

The fact of the matter is that flaming arrows can most certainly damage and hurt the protector. But let's not forget about the fallout. Consequences are serious. Few people live in isolation, and sin especially has consequences. God gives every believer the opportunity to pick up the shield of faith, not just for the believer himself but also for those the believer needs to shield.

I think of the devastating effects of alcohol. I know some believers whose greatest struggle in life pertains to this scourge. It's like a drug. Some people call it a sickness. Whatever your perspective or opinion, booze is a classic destroyer of homes, families, and lives. It is an instrument that Satan uses so well on college campuses, at business retreats, and across the board. Mother's Against Drunk Drivers (MADD) will tell you about the scourge of alcohol.

God's Word invites us to pick up the shield of faith so that we ourselves are protected as well as those entrusted to our protection, which, when you really think about it, sometimes is someone you don't even know. With the shield of faith firmly in hand, we can be stronger in our faith, determined in our walk, confident in our battles, and armed to the teeth when we encounter our enemies. It also gives those entrusted to us a solid wall to stand behind, a flag to follow, a hope to endure, and a future to look forward to.

2. *By pulling over (v. 17a).* Probably the most vulnerable part of the body is the head. The Old Testament tells the story of young David as his people faced the onslaught of the giant, Goliath. The Bible tells us Goliath was huge and mean to the core. The Israelites were so afraid of his power and might they were rendered useless, and there was little they could do about it. "When the Israelites saw the man, they all ran from him in great fear" (1 Sam. 17:24 NIV). Defeat was imminent, and the alarm bells were being sounded for the retreat, except for one thing. God was still on His throne! Nothing was too big for God, and He had a plan for every circumstance and every challenge in life. Just think of how small David must have looked to Goliath. Just think about the thunderous sounds of the Philistines as they watched and howled with laughter as this diminutive little chap walked out on to the field:

> David said to the Philistine, "You come against
> me with sword and spear and javelin, but
> I come against you in the name of the LORD
> Almighty, the God of the armies of Israel,
> whom you have defied. This day the LORD

will hand you over to me, and I'll strike you
down and cut off your head. Today I will give
the carcasses of the Philistine army to the birds
of the air and the beasts of the earth, and the
whole world will know that there is a God in
Israel. All those gathered here will know that it
is not by sword or spear that the LORD saves;
for the battle is the LORD's, and he will give all
of you into our hands." (1 Sam. 17:45–47 NIV)

This is why the helmet is so important. These pieces of
armor are not physical instruments. God is not asking you
to wear an actual helmet or pick up an actual shield. He is
giving us a spiritual resource that David was talking about.
Just as Goliath thought David's physical appearance and lack
of physical armor were indicative of his vulnerability, so it
is that Satan just doesn't get it. What Satan does get is what
Goliath did not get, that there was just enough room below
his physical helmet to slam home a missile in the form of a
small stone. That is all David needed. And that is all Satan
needs to slam home his missiles at you. God wants you to
wear his helmet of salvation because it will guarantee at least
two important things for you in the journey of life.

It guarantees the believer's total security in Christ. My men-
tor and friend, Dr. Billy Graham, encouraged me to write a
book entitled *Totally Secure.* I encourage you to get a copy.
In it God's Word is used to help us understand the deep
and lasting significance of knowing the Lord Jesus Christ
as Savior and Lord. This is what the helmet does for us.

The helmet of salvation is an essential part of God's armor because it serves as a constant and continual reminder that we belong to Jesus. The Bible teaches that we are totally secure in the hands of the Commander in Chief when we repent of our sin and trust Him by faith. No one can tear us away from Him, not even our Goliaths. This is why I love the passage in Hebrews in which the author cautions believers to pay close attention to the issue of salvation. He was talking to Christian people when he put it like this:

> We must pay more careful attention, therefore, to what we have heard, so that we do not drift away. For if the message spoken by angels was binding, and every violation and disobedience received its just punishment, how shall we escape if we ignore such a great salvation? This salvation, which was first announced by the Lord, was confirmed to us. . . . God also testified to it by signs, wonders and various miracles, and gifts of the Holy Spirit distributed according to his will. (Heb. 2:1–4 NIV)

The operative phrase here is "such a great salvation." The writer begins with a word of extreme caution. Watch out! Be careful that you do not neglect to pull the helmet of salvation over your head. Without it firmly in place, you will be exposed to the onslaught of the devil. With the helmet on your head, you will always be assured of the basic tenants of your salvation. The basic tenants of your salvation are binding in that the shed blood of the Lord Jesus Christ guarantees them. This guarantee covers every violation and every act of disobedience ever committed by man. Without this guarantee, the just punishment of a righteous and holy God would be handed down and spiritual death follows. Throughout the annals of human history and time, God has confirmed the abiding truth and validity of this guarantee by means of signs and wonders and various miracles, like the raising of the Lord Jesus from the dead. So don't neglect this great salvation. God has given it to you to wear about your head, and your head will know what your heart has experienced in Christ.

But there is a second and more compelling reason we must pull this helmet over our heads. It has to do with the way we serve the Lord.

It ensures the believer's service for Christ. When you accept God's offer concerning the helmet of salvation, at least six things will be ensured in your life:

You will run with perseverance. I love what we read in the book of Hebrews: "Therefore, since we are surrounded by such a great cloud of witnesses, let us throw off everything that hinders and the sin that so easily entangles, and let us run with perseverance the race marked out for us" (Heb. 12:1 NIV). What a powerful statement and what a powerful reminder for us as we face every known trial and tribulation in life. With the helmet of salvation firmly pulled over our heads, we find ourselves covered with the means by which we are able to persevere in the race of life. Many of us are simply exhausted in our own strength. I have often thought that Paul would never have said, "Fight the good fight of faith," if he did not believe there was a fight to fight! We are engaged in a battlefield, and the roaring lion is prowling around, actively engaged in a strategy to trip us up and break us down. However, we will not succumb with the helmet of salvation firmly installed on our heads.

You will fight with tenacity. Perhaps one of the greatest joys of my life is my grandson, Bolt! I just love him. What can I say? The day he was born at Oschner Hospital in New Orleans is a day I will never forget. He was born in the same city as his father and in the same hospital as his Aunt Shelley and on the same day his Auntie Shelley was born, only eighteen years later. Just watching Bolt grow is a delight to all of us. What is particularly cute to me is the way he holds up his little arms with his fists clenched in a boxing style. It's like he is punching the air with combination hooks and jabs that either speak of frustration at times or sheer joy on other occasions. In a similar way the onslaught of Satan makes us clench our fists and resort to shadow boxing in our hearts. The helmet of salvation serves to give us the shot of tenacity we need. The knowledge of our salvation brings to bear all that God has done for us in and through the Lord Jesus Christ. Too many of us are asking the wrong questions of God. It is not about what I can do for God as much as it is what God can do for me. This is not a cheeky question or being sassy with God. This is not being rude and arrogant either. It is about the finished work of the Lord Jesus Christ on the cross. It is about this incredible thing called salvation. This is about the most unbelievable act of God's mercy and grace "in that, while we were yet sinners, Christ Jesus died for us" (Rom. 5:8 KJV). Read this wonderful promise from God's Word:

> Do you not know that in a race all the runners
> run, but only one gets the prize? Run in such a
> way as to get the prize. Everyone who competes
> in the games goes into strict training. They do
> it to get a crown that will not last; but we do it
> to get a crown that will last forever. Therefore
> I do not run like a man running aimlessly; I do
> not fight like a man beating the air. No, I beat
> my body and make it my slave so that after
> I have preached to others, I myself will not be
> disqualified for the prize. (1 Cor. 9:24–27 NIV)

You will serve with endurance. When one considers his upbringing, his story is even more remarkable. We can't even imagine the luxury of Pharaoh's court. Moses had it all except for one thing; he had settled the issue of whom he belonged to. This is why he refused to be called the son of Pharaoh's daughter when he came of age. He knew he was a child of the King of kings and Lord of lords, even though his grandfather had a different opinion. And once he had made his choice, he stuck with it despite the opposition. He was even willing to suffer disgrace by throwing his lot in with God's people rather than to enjoy the worldly pleasures offered him at every turn in the road. And once he had settled these issues, he knew what he needed to do. The option was distinct and clear. It was, in fact, not an option. He had to leave Egypt. He realized he could not serve both God and man at the same time. God had commissioned him, and God had told him to pack his bags and move on, and pack his bags and move on he did.

God has blessed my family in many ways because we have been willing to endure and keep on keeping on. This is not, in any way, to suggest that we have led perfect lives. Far be it. Like you, we are sinners saved by the grace of God alone! But my story may serve to inspire you just as others stories of endurance have inspired me. Remember, "Iron sharpens iron."

It began with my mom and dad, John and Rhodabelle Wilton. After they gave their hearts and lives to the Lord Jesus, the thought of not leaving their hometown and business to follow the Lord's call into ministry was just not an option. God called them into full-time gospel ministry. Throughout their wonderful life and ministry I can't even imagine the challenges they faced. They experienced everything from poverty, to the challenges of ministry, to one difficult middle son when he was a teenager, to the answering of God's call to move from one place of service to another. In their midfifties God called them to leave the country they love and come to the United States of America. I remember standing on the banks of the mighty Mississippi River in White Castle, Louisiana, and chatting with my parents about starting all over again in America. They arrived with little but the helmet of salvation and armor of God in their suitcases. Today they are full of the joy of the Lord Jesus and continue to serve in the fullness of His grace and mercy. No son could be more blessed!

It also began with my parents-in-law, Ed and Mirth Bolton. My father-in-law was a successful businessman with a wonderful family and a bright and promising future. But God called them into full-time gospel ministry. They gave it all up and followed our Savior. Over the years their ministry has been marked by an uncommon faithfulness and endurance that surely has pleased the heart of God. They, too, have faced every known challenge. They have served in such small churches one wonders how they could ever have survived. They have listened to more people's problems than I could ever imagine and have faced every known struggle of mankind. Most significantly they have faced the untimely death of their eldest daughter who drowned tragically as a young girl. And yet they have endured. In their midfifties God gave them the opportunity to join their children in the United States of America. They forsook all they knew and loved and followed the Lord's invitation. To change home and country at their age requires a special determination and discipline, but they did it with their heads held high. They faced a different culture and different food; they faced a different way of doing church and a different mind-set when it comes to many things that are important to us all. But they endured, and today they serve the Lord with hearts full of gladness and joy. I do not believe I have ever seen them as happy as they are today.

The greatest thing about the Boltons was that they gave me a beautiful wife. God used their daughter to change my life and give it new meaning and a new hope and future, grounded in the promises of God. From the day I first laid my eyes on her, I could not tear them away. She knew to whom she belonged, and she knew what she believed. By His Spirit, she had seen the one who is invisible, and she knew what she had to do. After I settled the issue of my own personal relationship with the Lord Jesus Christ, it was my wife who confirmed God's call for us to forsake all and follow him. With promising careers well on the road and the hope of a bright future sparkling in our eyes, we realized the Lord had no intention for us to be the sons of Pharaoh's daughter. My wife was willing to sell most of her prized possessions, including treasured wedding gifts, just to garner enough money to pay back government loans and buy two tickets to the United States of America. My wife was the one who was willing to begin a new life with nothing but two suitcases and $1400 in our pockets. My wife was the one who, time without number, kicked me (gently) in the pants, encouraged me to study hard, preach with all my heart, paint the seminary campus as though my life depended on it, and love God's people with no strings attached. I have watched her put up with so much junk from church people, and I have watched her pack her bags and move every time the Lord told us to do so. I have watched Karyn love both sets of parents equally and with an undivided heart of compassion and responsibility. I have stood and watched her bring up our two sons and our daughter to the point at which the proof is in the pudding! I have heard her speak with such wisdom it would confound the members of the Sanhedrin, and yet with such passion that it would convert the Rock of Gibraltar.

But it does not stop there. When God gets a hold of you, He will pass it on from one generation to the next. It has amazed me how both my brothers forsook lucrative careers to follow the Lord Jesus just as our dad has done. And it leaves both Karyn and me in breathless wonder as we watch our sons, Rob and Greg, follow after the heart of God with such passion.

It really is amazing when you think about it. And it all began because our parents were willing to take hold of the helmet of salvation. What God does when just one man or one woman gives his or her heart to Jesus defies human understanding. Prior to my dad's conversion, we are not aware of any person in our extended family that had a personal relationship with the Lord Jesus. There may well have been, and I'm sure there were, but we do not know about it. I do not see any fruit and can find no evidence. But since the day my dad surrendered to the lordship of Christ, we can humbly find literally hundreds, if not thousands, of people, whose lives have never been the same because they have taken a drink of the Living Water. These are the scores of people who today have a hope and a future. I'll let God's Word have the final say concerning the issue of endurance.

You then, my son, be strong in the grace
that is in Christ Jesus. And the things you
have heard me say in the presence of many
witnesses entrust to reliable men who will also
be qualified to teach others. Endure hardship
with us like a good soldier of Christ Jesus. No
one serving as a soldier gets involved in civilian
affairs—he wants to please his commanding
officer. Similarly, if anyone competes as an
athlete, he does not receive the victor's crown
unless he competes according to the rules.
The hardworking farmer should be the first to
receive the share of the crops. Reflect on what
I am saying, for the Lord will give you insight
into all this. (2 Tim. 2:1–7 NIV)

You will act with care. Foolish behavior gets even the best of us into trouble. Let's face it, we are quick to blame others and circumstances for almost every kind of woe and difficulty we face, and to some extent this is true. Probably on a scale of one to ten, the majority of junk we face and the discouragement we encounter comes from others. Satan leads the pack, but there are also mitigating circumstances, like poverty and lack of education, that certainly cause great stress and hardship in many lives. So we are not trying to discount the majority, but my father always taught me an important principle. When I point my finger at the congregation when preaching, I do well to remember that three fingers are pointing right back at me!

When Titus, Paul's "true son in our common faith," received his letter, he read about a whole lot of important things, including the admonition to be careful about his own conduct.

> This is a trustworthy saying. And I want
> you to stress these things, so that those who
> have trusted in God may be careful to devote
> themselves to doing what is good. These things
> are excellent and profitable for everyone.
> (Titus 3:8 NIV)

I believe Titus was being admonished to lead the way in his training of others and to live a life himself that would be pleasing to the Lord. To be honest, there are many times when others are not to blame for our disappointments and discouragements. We are! Our own behavior is the real problem.

I remember preaching in a local church revival where the pastor was quick to tell me just how sorry his people were. He went on and on about their lack of this and their attitude toward that. But I soon realized that he was the problem. This man was insecure and had an attitude about everything, including the noonday sun. In three days of services I never heard him say one kind word to anybody in his congregation. He seemed to have a big chip on his shoulder. I don't think I could have put up with him if I went to that church.

Another preacher was quick to lament the condition of his marriage. His wife was not on board with him in the ministry. He loved her and she loved him, but it seemed like she was always unhappy with him. When I observed the way he treated her, I realized why she had a problem. He had a quick and ready smile for any and all in his church. He could turn on the charm in a heartbeat. On one particular occasion, he had just finished speaking warmly and affectionately to someone who had come up to him after the service when his wife walked up and gently asked if he knew where they were going to eat. He turned on her in front of everyone and verbally demeaned her to the point that she literally crept away like a whipped puppy. You could see the hurt on the faces of the people.

This is another good reason we need to pull the helmet of salvation firmly over our heads. Without it we will act in an unseemly manner and bring great discredit to the cause of Christ.

You will operate with humility. Without the helmet of salvation, we have one big serious problem. Peter put it like this: "All of you, clothe yourselves with humility toward one another, because, 'God opposes the proud but gives grace to the humble'" (1 Pet. 5:5 NIV).

It has been said that the closer you get to some people the more you realize they have clay feet.

It has been one of the joys of my life to sit at the feet of Dr. Billy Graham. The first time I was invited to visit with him and Ruth in Montreat will always be etched into my heart and memory. I was nervous as one of his men drove up the steep and winding road, passed the home of dear

George Beverly Shea and through the gate to the Graham's home. The last few feet left my heart pounding in my chest. I was not sure how I should speak, what I should say, or how I should act in the presence of this man who had been used so mightily of the Lord Jesus to touch millions of people for Christ. As the car drew up to the side entrance of his home, out of the door came both Billy and his wife. He was dressed in a blue sweater and had on a pair of blue jeans. He was surrounded by a bunch of dogs that seemed to love his every move. Mrs. Graham was right there with him as he walked up and literally opened my car door. In an instant I felt as though Billy Graham had been misinformed about who I was. Everything seemed backward. An outside observer would have concluded that I was a prince or prime minister. My world was turned upside down. There was suddenly no need for me to remember my lines.

The humility of Billy Graham is one thing I cherish about this dear man. And it has never changed. Every time we visit, he is just the same. He always makes me feel like the honored guest. As I sit at his feet, I always feel as though I am sitting at the feet of the Lord Jesus, which is so ironic because that is the last thing Mr. Graham would ever want me to say about him. He has talked to me and shared his life with me in a way that I have never fully comprehended. I will never get over the fact that he regards me as his pastor and friend. Even though he may not feel well, when I am with him, he makes me feel as though I am his prime concern. His body is now full of pain, and his hearing is nearly gone, and yet he has reached out his trembling hand and touched me and asked if I would mind if he prayed for me! It is amazing how someone who has done so much in his life can be so humble. The Lord Jesus Christ does that for us!

The greatest thing we can do to be truly humble in spirit and attitude is to do what the Lord Jesus tells us to do. We must pull the helmet of salvation tightly over our heads.

You will seek God with reverence. The helmet of salvation not only guarantees the believer's total security in Christ but also ensures the believer's service for Christ. It means that you and I can stand up and be counted for the Lord as we serve Him with perseverance, tenacity, endurance, care, humility, and reverence. Open your heart to the following wonderful words:

> Since we have these promises, dear friends,
> let us purify ourselves from everything that
> contaminates body and spirit, perfecting
> holiness out of reverence for God.
> (2 Cor. 7:1 NIV)

What a powerful word! This great salvation we have in Christ is our source of inspiration and motivation. It inspires us in the middle of the battlefield to stand up straight and defy the odds, while at the same time it motivates us to bow in the presence of the One who is Lord of all. God's salvation carries with it the guarantees of the heart of God's promises that we have available to us in Christ.

This is what Paul is referring to in this wonderful passage. Because of this it is imperative that we are armed with the helmet of salvation every day of our lives. It will serve as a constant reminder to "come out from them and be separate" (2 Cor. 6:17 NIV), and be counted as one who belongs to the Lord, no matter what our circumstances in life. Talk about strength for the journey! Our reverence for God will help us "purify ourselves from everything that contaminates [the] body" (2 Cor. 7:1 NIV). Our reverence for God fortifies us in our weakness.

In short, God wants us to have available protection by picking up the shield of faith and by pulling over the helmet of salvation. There is one final action that needs to be taken in order to be protected adequately in the journey of life.

3. By holding up (v. 17b). I love this final piece of equipment. The Roman soldier had a clear understanding of the significance of the sword. He knew what would happen to him if he went anywhere without his sword. He would not stand a chance of survival. Furthermore, he knew that it was not necessarily good enough simply to have the sword in its sheath. It would be like a gun without bullets in it when you needed to defend yourself. The soldier would also know that even if he had the sword in his hand he would need to hold it up in the ready position. He needed to be ready to strike. Even boxers will tell you the best time to land a good punch on your opponent is when he drops his hands.

Back in their day, these swords were between six and eighteen inches long. The spiritual sword of the Spirit is the Word of God. This sword defies human understanding and can never be measured in feet and inches. Here are two major reasons the sword of the Spirit is such a critical part of a believer's arsenal.

Why We Must Hold On to the Sword

1. It is specific in origin. When Paul wrote to Timothy, he placed the origin of the Word of God squarely at the feet of our heavenly Father. He encouraged his "son" in the faith to take a stand against evil men and imposters who were out to sidetrack and destroy everything Timothy believed in.

> In fact, everyone who wants to live a godly
> life in Christ Jesus will be persecuted, while
> evil men and imposters will go from bad to
> worse, deceiving and being deceived. But as
> for you, continue in what you have learned
> and have become convinced of, because you
> know those from whom you learned it, and
> how from infancy you have known the holy
> Scriptures, which are able to make you wise
> for salvation through faith in Christ Jesus. All
> Scripture is God-breathed and is useful for
> teaching, rebuking, correcting and training in
> righteousness, so that the man of God may
> be thoroughly equipped for every good work.
> (2 Tim. 3:12–17 NIV)

This was a direct reminder to hold on to the sword of the Spirit because of its roots that are deep and abiding. You may remember when Hurricane Gustav approached the Louisiana coastline. Fear gripped the hearts of millions of people because they knew what Hurricane Katrina had done to them exactly three years earlier. Besides, by the time it arrived just west of Grand Isle, it had already built a killer reputation. Reports released were confirming more than eighty-five deaths in Haiti, the Dominican Republic, and other Caribbean Islands. Cuba had been devastated just west of Havana, but the death toll had not been made known. What was known was that the lives of numbers of impoverished people must have been altered in ways few could ever have imagined. By the time it reached the United States, the governor of Louisiana and the mayors of cities and towns from Alabama to Mississippi and Texas had issued orders for residents to evacuate their homes. Vehicles jammed the highways and interstates as people headed to safety.

But many defied the order. One such man was the owner of a seafood restaurant on Grand Isle, Louisiana. Fox News showed the sheriff of that small town driving his truck around in an effort to make sure his people had complied with the mandatory evacuation. The mayor of New Orleans made the statement that anyone who did not comply would "be on his or her own." My own sons, Rob and Greg, complied. Greg headed for South Florida to be with his fiancée, Abby, while Rob sent Annabeth and my grandson, Bolt, to be with his grandparents in South Carolina. Initially, Rob and a group of young men determined to stay and stick it out so that they could help those who could not help themselves. Most of all, they wanted to use the opportunity to be witnesses for Jesus Christ. But when he realized just how dangerous the storm had become and the potential havoc it could wreak on New Orleans, they headed over the Pontchartrain causeway to the north shore and Covington, Louisiana, where they hunkered down to ride the storm out.

But not the man on Grand Isle. In an interview with the press, he referred to the strength of his home. The pillars and beams, he said, ran deep into the ground.

This is what Paul is trying to tell Timothy and God is saying to all of us. We will face every kind of persecution known to man. Trials and tribulations will occur. Any person who makes an effort to lead a godly life will face an onslaught from evil men and imposters. You will become discouraged and depressed. You will be tossed about in the wind. The hurricanes will blow through your heart and home and will cause great destruction. But you can trust the sword of the Spirit!

Here are some important things to note regarding its use:

- Hold God's Word close to you at all times.
- Hold God's Word in your heart at all times.
- Hold God's Word up at all times.

2. It is faultless in content. I don't know about you, but I want to be able to rely on the things I believe in so deeply. With the sword of the Spirit held firmly in hand, we have a resource that is faultless in content. Read what the psalmist had to say about this:

> The law of the LORD is perfect,
> reviving the soul.
> The statutes of the LORD are trustworthy,
> making the wise simple.
> The precepts of the LORD are right,
> giving joy to the heart.
> The commands of the LORD are radiant,
> giving light to the eyes.
> (Ps. 19:7–8 NIV)

Note the four designated names given to the Scriptures. God's Word is called *the law, the statutes, the precepts,* and *the commands.* It follows that the person who holds on to the sword of the Spirit has in their hand/heart four life anchors that guarantee a hope and a future. People who are harnessed to these four anchors literally and spiritually have a vehicle in which to navigate the storms and stresses of life.

The Four Anchors of the Sword of the Spirit

1. The law. This can also be translated "His teaching," "a direction," or "instruction." This means the Word of God bears testimony to its Divine Author. The root word is the same word from which we get our words "to bear testimony" or "to provide evidence on behalf of someone else." This is why the psalmist let it be known:

> Blessed is the man who does not walk in the
> counsel of the wicked or stand in the way of
> sinners or sit in the seat of mockers. But his
> delight is in the law of the LORD, and on his
> law he mediates day and night. He is like a tree
> planted by streams of water, which yields its
> fruit in season and whose leaf does not wither.
> Whatever he does prospers. (Ps. 1:1–3 NIV)

Anchor number one means I am holding on to the Author and Finisher of my life as I journey through this life. What a hope and what a future!

2. The statutes. Just as law enforcement officials inform a speeding motorist what the legal orders are concerning a speed limit, so it is that God's Word is the command center concerning the governance of God's law. The word *statutes* is really a synonym that looks on God's Word as a set of "orders," charges and precepts that are designed by God alone to command all that we need to do in life. Without these statutes, we are left to our own devices and have nothing to ground our behavior or to give us the instructions we need to follow. No wonder Paul insisted we hold on to "the sword of the Spirit" (Eph. 6:17). Don't let it get out of your hand!

3. The precepts. Whereas statutes refer to a set of orders, the anchor presented by this word refers more to an injunction concerning moral conduct. It carries with it the idea of technical detail in the carrying out of the law of God. I like to think of it as the practical means by which I am anchored in my faith because precepts are the application of the law and statutes of God through His Word.

I realize this may be difficult to grasp and fully understand, but I implore you to think about this. When it comes to the sword of the Spirit, we must work through our understanding because it is so important. Let me put it this way when it comes to the first three anchors.

God has given us His Word, which Paul calls the sword of the Spirit. When we hold on to this sword, we are holding on to God's written set of orders (the Law), by which we are encouraged (the statutes) to carry out the precepts as we apply them to our lives, so that we can be radiant and complete because we have obeyed the commands of the Lord.

4. The commands. A command is an order given by a person who has the authority to give an order. It carries with it the idea of control and ownership. It also paints a picture of a garrison of soldiers all gathered under the command of their superior officer. One of the most frequent complaints one hears from head coaches in the National Football League pertains to this issue. The issues are so big in the league, and egos are so massive that many coaches feel they cannot effectively organize their teams to win if they do not have absolute authority over their players. And given the huge salaries and the professional nature of the sport, one can understand how difficult it must be to have a team in which one or two players believe they are above the authority of the head coach.

When it comes to God, football coaches are not even on the radar screen. Life is not just a game, although some people may think it is. And football is not life. It is just a game. But this life we live here on this earth is serious business. God created us and made us for the express purpose of having an intimate and personal relationship with Him. Nothing in the Bible suggests the Christian life is a cruise around the Mediterranean. Life is full of hazards of the highest order. One hurricane after another is guaranteed to blow through our hearts and lives, sometimes with devastating effect. But Jesus has promised, "I have come that they may have life, and have it to the full" (John 10:10 NIV).

We must obey His commands. And His commands come through His Word. Obedience to His commands is, in fact, a hallmark of salvation. Obedience confirms that we actually do belong to the Lord Jesus Christ. The apostle John made this point when he wrote the following words:

> We know that we have come to know him
> if we obey his commands. The man who
> says, "I know him," but does not do what he
> commands is a liar, and the truth is not in him.
> But if anyone obeys his word, God's love is
> truly made complete in him. This is how we

know we are in him: Whoever claims to live in
him must walk as Jesus did. (1 John 2:3–6 NIV)

This fourth anchor presented to us is where the water
hits the wheel. It is like the old proverbial saying, "You can
lead a horse to the water, but you can't make him drink."
Every individual has to examine his or her own heart in this
regard. This is not an option.

Here we have the sword of the Spirit described as the
anchor. I personally love this description because this is
the anchor that will hold when the storms of life toss us to
and fro in the wind.

But this is still incomplete. There is more to the faultless content of the Word of God. We have taken a look at
the four anchors of God's Word that root us to our Savior.
Each of these anchors carries an attribute most worthy of
consideration. These attributes describe what His Word is;
each is a pronouncement of what God's Word effectively
is in character. And if you and I understand the essential
character of God's Word, we will have an asset in our hands
that defies human understanding. The four attributes are
perfection, trustworthiness, rightness, and radiance. They
produce revival, wisdom, joy, and light.

The Four Attributes of the Sword of the Spirit

1. Perfection. Herein lies the heart of who God is by virtue of His divine character. He is perfect in every way, and

this is directly reflected through His Word. As such, God's Word represents the highest state of proficiency, skill, and excellence. It is the perfect embodiment and example of all God is in His eternal sovereignty. It follows that the holder of the sword of the Spirit is one who has access to the highest skill necessary to combat any and all situations in life.

The perfection of the sword of the Spirit revives both the heart and soul-spirit of the believer. The relentless battering that so many take from the course of life leaves many exhausted and exasperated.

To revive someone means to bring that person back to life. And you can only revive something or someone who has an element of life in them to begin with. What the psalmist is saying at this point is that God's law is perfect in every way and, as such, has the capability and capacity to bring back to life that which may have been impacted to the point of uselessness. This is how the soul is revived. How can we possibly afford to live this life without holding firmly to the sword of the Spirit?

2. Trustworthiness. The psalmist tells us that the statutes of the Lord are trustworthy. When we are armed with God's sword, we have every right to consider all of his instructions and orders as completely trustworthy. Trustworthiness is one of the many missing ingredients in life. If trust is the reliance on the integrity, strength, ability, or surety of a person or thing, then spiritual trust must be the absolute reliance we can have in all that God has to say to us in and through His Word. When trust is placed *in* someone, then it follows that the one placing that trust is, in fact, leaving his or her "valuables" in the safest hands possible. The United States of America, I believe, suffers from misplaced and misguided trust. We claim the caption, "In God We Trust" on our currency, but we seldom practice this trust as a people. In this case we, the people, are at fault, not God. God cannot change this attribute. His character is eternal, timeless, and inextricably intertwined in the heart and the holiness of who He is.

And so it is with the sword of the Spirit. The injunction here is to "take hold" of something that is totally reliable in every way—without exception. Trustworthiness not only refers to the one who is worthy of receiving all of our trust but also to the ones who are the receivers of that trust. And that is you and I. However, here is the clincher. The product of these reliable statutes is wisdom! Boy, do we need bags full of wisdom as we try to walk through the challenges of this life. How many times do we not hear ourselves pleading for wisdom? "Lord help me," we cry out. "What do I do now?" "How can I respond to this situation or to this person?" "I don't know what to do next."

Help is not only on the way, but it is right there in the pages of God's Word. Hold on to it because it is faultless in content!

3. Rightness. In a world that increasingly compromises, we find more and more people hovering between two opinions. Our young people often find themselves caught between a rock and a hard place. To be "right" about something means to be fully in accordance with that which is good or proper or just. It means correctness according to an absolute, not simply according to an opinion. The Word of God carries the fundamental arm of all that a Christian ought to believe.

This third attribute of rightness puts the perspective of absolute truth in its proper place. It restores or puts in place the only issue that stands in an upright position. With the sword of the Spirit held firmly in hand and heart, the Christian soldier is fully armed with the absoluteness that comes with the authority of God Almighty. Talk about the American Express credit card—you can't leave home without the trustworthiness of the statutes of the Lord, and as a result they will produce pure joy!

Think about this for a second. What is the one thing that suffers as much as any other when you come under attack from the enemy? Joy and happiness seem to take a hike down the road! Life, in fact, can become miserable at times when the battle is raging. I have met few Christian friends who have looked at me and said, "Oh, whoop-de-do, I'm under attack and want you to know just how happy I am right now!" This third attribute certainly highlights the faultless content of the sword of the Spirit.

4. Radiance. This fourth attribute of God's Word is simply terrific. Webster defines *radiance* in an adjectival sense as that which "emits rays of light." This has to be classified as something or someone who brings forth warmth and provides light. Radiance shows the ways in the dark and guides the lost. This attribute is most perfectly applied to the Lord Jesus who is described as "the radiance of God's glory" (Heb. 1:3 NIV). The word *radiance* or *brightness* is used in the New Testament only on this one occasion. It expresses the concept of sending forth light and carries the idea of something that shines brilliantly. In 2 Corinthians Paul makes this same point when he talks about the mission of the Lord Jesus:

> And even if our gospel is veiled, it is veiled to those who are perishing. The god of this age has blinded the minds of unbelievers, so that they cannot see the light of the gospel of the glory of Christ, who is the image of God. For we do not preach ourselves, but Jesus Christ as Lord, and ourselves as your servants for Jesus' sake. For God, who said, "Let light shine out of darkness," made his light shine in our hearts to give us the light of the knowledge of the glory of God in the face of Christ. (2 Cor. 4:3–6 NIV)

Jesus validated this attribute Himself when He spoke to the people: "I am the light of the world. Whoever follows me will never walk in darkness, but will have the light of life" (John 8:12). The Lord Jesus is never called a reflection of God because a reflection would water down the fact of His being God. The Son is not simply reflecting the glory of God the Father. He is the exact, express image of the Father making Him the perfect imprint and the exact representation of the nature and essence of God in time and space.

If the commands of the Lord are attributed with radiance, then the product of this attribute is the giving of light. One's eyes become the beneficiary of radiance both literally and spiritually. The eyes benefit literally in that God enables His children to see what is going on around them. Remember how important it is to open your eyes even in the middle of your battlefield. More importantly, God enables you to see with spiritual eyes when you are holding on to the sword of the Spirit. This means you are able to interpret life's data through spiritual eyes. Your spiritual perception acts as a filter through which you are able to make judgments and determine responses. As a result your whole perspective changes when things are seen from an eternal perspective and not always from an earthly perspective.

This is truly amazing and wonderful. When we take hold of God's Word, we are given something of enormous value because it is specific in origin and it is faultless in content. But the sword of the Spirit is also complete in revelation.

Chapter Five

I Am Going to Stay
in the Boat

Perhaps the greatest fallout of discouragement is the compulsion to quit! And who can blame you? Many people find it somewhat easy to offer all kinds of advice to those who are hurting, but it is another thing altogether to find oneself in the middle of the storm. I remember preaching at Ridgecrest Baptist Conference Center in Black Mountain, North Carolina, many years ago when I encountered a young man who had decided to quit. I came across him, or he came across me, quite by accident, although I am convinced the Lord Jesus allowed him to see me in the dark that night.

As I put my arm around his sobbing shoulders, he began to tell me his story. His parents had divorced, and he had grown up in a conflict-filled home. Few peers wanted to befriend him, and his rather awkward looks did not make matters any easier. Girls had little interest in him and often giggled when he passed by. Loneliness was his constant companion, and a feeling of uselessness reared its ugly head in his life. That was the night he heard about the love of the Lord Jesus Christ in a meaningful way, but things were coming to a head. He told me he would be better off dead! I am glad to report I was able to help stabilize his suicidal thoughts and then get him some real help. I am told he pulled through and really turned a corner. I trust he is doing well today and commend him to the grace of God.

There are millions of people just like this young boy. I suggest "millions" because "thousands" would be a gross underestimate. As the pastor of just one congregation, I see and hear of more cases of apparent hopelessness and helplessness than one could ever imagine. The inclination to "abandon ship" is not only out there; it is real and understandable.

Jesus' disciples had an experience with the Lord Jesus in a boat. This story began with a large crowd pressing to get alongside the Savior. Evidently they had heard the news, and many of them had borne witness to the miracles Jesus was performing. They knew He was the one who could do for them what they could not do for themselves. He had the answer, and they were determined to get it from Him.

So they followed Him everywhere He went. This is where we pick up the story:

> When Jesus saw large crowds around Him, He
> gave the order to go to the other side of the
> sea. . . . As He got into the boat, His disciples
> followed Him. Suddenly, a violent storm arose
> on the sea, so that the boat was being swamped
> by the waves. But He was sleeping. So the
> disciples came and woke Him up, saying,
> "Lord, save us! We're going to die!"
>
> But He said to them, "Why are you fearful,
> you of little faith?" Then He got up and
> rebuked the winds and the sea. And there was a
> great calm.
>
> The men were amazed and asked, "What
> kind of man is this?—even the winds and the
> sea obey Him!" (Matt. 8:18, 23–27)

What an incredible story! Now let's think about how this can be applied to our own lives. I want you to see life, symbolically, as a boat. There is a sense in which all of us are sailing across the sea in the confines of our own situations and circumstances. Four major principles provide the floorboard of our "boat." The facts are that God *is*, in that He is sovereign and rules over this world in every way; God *knows*, in that He is all knowing; God *loves*, in that He gave His only Son to die on the cross for our sin and then seeks us out to give our hearts and lives to Him. And the final principle, God *cares,* in that He sustains us through the journey of life. So the boat we find ourselves in is handmade by God Himself. It is not going to sink, and the Lord Jesus Christ is on board.

With these principles in mind there are eight important things to note about this dramatic encounter with the Lord Jesus in the boat:

1. Jesus climbed aboard before the storm hit (v. 23). So many Christians were praying before Hurricanes Camille, Katrina, Hugo, Gustav, and all the others came ashore. The reason was simple and yet profound. Believers know that God will never leave and never forsake us, in part because He is there from the beginning. God does not "roam" around like Satan does. He is omnipresent, which means He is everywhere all the time. He is actively engaged in the affairs of man all the time. He never steps out of the boat or takes a break to tend to other matters. The Bible speaks of Satan's roaming around over the earth when he was speaking to God about Job. God doesn't have to roam. He simply is everywhere, all the time.

> One day the sons of God came again to present themselves before the LORD, and Satan also came with them to present himself before the LORD. The LORD asked Satan, "Where have you come from?"
>
> "From roaming through the earth," Satan answered Him, "and walking around on it." (Job 2:1–2)

The Lord Jesus climbed aboard the boat before the storm arrived. Of course, during Jesus' day there were no radar systems or qualified meteorologists to warn them of a pending storm. In our world today, we know of the possibilities days ahead of the actual touchdown. We have plenty of time to get ready and evacuate if needed, but this was not so for the disciples. They had no idea. This can be so much like our own lives and circumstances. While many of us can be warned and prepared, many have little warning. Many are suddenly diagnosed "out of the blue" and find themselves plunged into every kind of predicament known to man. It is so encouraging to know that the Lord Jesus Christ is already on board.

2. The men followed without discussion. Now this is a tough one. However, it is critical to understand. Here we find this group of followers who knew and loved the Lord Jesus but were filled with so much junk at every turn. Any observer would have noticed how they jostled for position, argued about everything, debated among themselves, and acted as though they were God's appointed federal agents assigned to protect the president from any harm and danger. Jesus invested His life into the training of these twelve disciples, and this was one of those occasions when His investment paid off. Initially, at least! Some might suggest the disciples were singled out for special treatment because they were the ones who were able to get into the boat with Jesus, and I think they may be right. Jesus treats us all like this. He wants us to be in the boat with Him and to get on board without discussion. This is one of those times when you don't need a deacons' meeting to decide what to do. Just get on board. There is no need to discuss who sits where and why the need has arisen or why all the others were not invited. Just get on board. Do you want to be in the boat with Jesus, or would you prefer just to stand on the shore and watch Him pass by?

I love the apparent silence here. See this bunch of talkers reduced to silence in the face of the one who is in the boat. Symbolically speaking, they climbed aboard those four principles we were talking about. When they boarded the boat, they found themselves standing on the fact that God is, God knows, God loves, and God cares! What more could any person want.

I was shown a video clip the other day that had made its way onto someone's Facebook page. A group of our young people, led by my friend Scott Brisken, crept into our home the day we first moved into it many years ago, aided by our sons who secretly opened the door unbeknown to us. They caught my wife, our little girl, and me still sleeping in bed together. It was such a funny video and reminded me of the way Shelley used to love to come and jump into our bed with us when she was a little girl. There were no questions and no discussions about it that I recall. She just knew that was the place to be at night. Mom and Dad were in there with her, and that was all that mattered. Osama Bin Laden himself could have come into the house for all she cared! No monster, and certainly no maniac, was even a thought to her when she was in the same boat with her mommy and daddy.

Perhaps you are asking too many questions. Perhaps you are hesitating too long. Perhaps you are full of junk and always need to have a debate before you jump on board with God. I don't know what you are up to, but this one thing I know, these men followed Jesus without discussion.

3. The storm came up without warning (v. 24). The little word *suddenly* carries a powerful punch! It literally means "without warning" and reminds me of the day I went fishing with my father-in-law. We all call him Bumpa, which I think is the greatest grandpa name ever.

After we had collected all our fishing gear, we drove down the road to the Swartkops River near Port Elizabeth, South Africa. The fishing was usually great there, and many grunter and other species had been pulled out of the river mouth as it fed itself into the Indian Ocean at Blue Water Bay. The day was a little overcast, making it ideal for a big catch. Our friend Jack had loaned us his boat and outboard motor, and soon we were chugging along happily in the water headed to the spot where Bumpa was convinced the fish were feeding.

Suddenly a violent storm came up that was frightening to experience. Our motor stuttered and stalled as the rain pelted down at right angles. The wind howled and the waves tossed the little boat about like a matchstick. We knew we were going under, and there was little we could do about it. The rain was so heavy we could not see the shoreline. To this day I can still see Bumpa with a big bucket in hand desperately bailing one bucket after another over the side of the boat, while yours truly stood on the bow of the boat with the anchor swirling around my head like a cowboy trying to rope a steer. I would literally hurl the anchor out into the angry water, wait for it to drop to the riverbed floor, and then begin to "reel" it in toward where I was desperately trying to hold on. Inch by inch we made forward progress until, almost totally exhausted, we reached the riverbank and safety.

The storms of life can come up suddenly just like this. It happened to the disciples after they followed Jesus into the boat, which brings up another important point. When you give your heart and life to the Lord Jesus, you do not become exempt from the storms of life. Just read the Beatitudes again or study the lives of so many of God's servants through-out the Scriptures. From the time of Adam's sin in the garden of Eden to the martyrdom of Stephen, we read about struggles of every kind. Just make sure you are in the boat with Jesus because these storms can pop up quickly; and if you are not in the boat, you are on your own!

4. *The waves swamped the boat (v. 24)*. The word *swamped* means the boat was literally inundated with water. It was bombarded and overcome in every way. It carries with it the idea of a military camp overrun by the enemy. This means the assault was complete, and everything at the disposal of the enemy was thrown into the attack. Just recently a lady said to me, "I cannot do this anymore!" She had reached the end of the line and had nothing else to give. Her reserves had completely run out of juice, and she was bone dry!

The point Jesus is making here is that we must not allow the enemy to dupe us into thinking his power is not all consuming. The enemy wants us to think that he is like a cute little puppy dog that simply yaps at the heels of some unfortunate passersby who finds himself or herself in the wrong place at the wrong time. I don't know how many times I have heard parents say something like, "Well boys will be boys you know!" in order to minimize the facts of their actions and activities. People who play with fire will get burned, that's for certain!

5. *The Son of Man was fast asleep (v. 24).* Perhaps a deeper understanding of who Jesus really was at this point is needed. In my book *When God Prayed*, I take a detailed look at Jesus' prayer in John 17. In it we find our Savior, just shortly before the agony of the cross, pouring His heart out to the Father. As He prayed, we hear the precious words of the Son in His capacity as the Son of Man. Jesus had come to this earth and had taken on Himself the sin of the world, even though He knew no sin Himself. We also know that our Savior lived on this earth fully as man in every way. He experienced pain, anguish, suffering, weariness, hunger, and the list goes on.

There was never a point at which the Lord Jesus ceased being God. When He came to this earth, He simply laid aside the privilege that was His from before the foundation of the world, as He took on human flesh. When His hour had come and it was God's time for the Son to go to the cross, Jesus prayed, "I have glorified You on the earth by completing the work You gave Me to do. Now, Father, glorify Me in Your presence with that glory I had with You before the world existed" (John 17:4–5). Hence my contention: *When God Prayed*. While we are listening to Jesus, pray we are also hearing God pray because Jesus told His disciples repeatedly, "I and the Father are one. If you have seen Me, you have seen the Father which is in heaven."

Jesus is asleep. What consternation there must have been in the boat! The storm was raging, their lives were in jeopardy, and Jesus was asleep. Or was He?

This is where our faith and actions collide. What we believe has a direct bearing on how we will act. A dear retired Methodist pastor and friend was chatting with me one day in Vermont. He reminded me of the extraordinary life of John Wesley, one of the founders of the Methodist church. I was fascinated as he reminded me of the time Wesley came to America with the express purpose of evangelizing the Indians. In a short time he realized he was serving God but was not a converted man himself. His life had not been transformed by the power of God to salvation. In the 1730s he boarded a ship and returned to England. Accompanying him on the journey were a number of Moravian missionaries returning to England as well. A bad storm arose to the point at which their lives were in serious jeopardy. John Wesley noticed how calm all the Moravians were even though their lives were threatened. He turned to a man named Peter Bohler to ask him why his people were so calm in the middle of the storm. Peter Bohler replied, "Do you have no faith, sir?"

John Wesley returned safely to England and soon thereafter attended a church meeting. During the worship service Wesley noted, "His heart was strangely warmed," and he was converted to a living faith and trust in Jesus Christ.

6. *The Son of God was fully awake (v. 25).* There is never a time, ever, that God goes to sleep. And if Jesus is God, then there was no way He was asleep. The fact is, God doesn't even need to sleep. He never takes time out, time off, and never has the need to take a vacation. God is always in our hearts and lives. He is ever present and is always actively engaged with us in our journeys of life.

These men found themselves in a dire predicament and probably could not believe that the Lord Jesus was asleep when they needed Him most. I think Jesus simply wanted to put them in their places. He wanted to force them to exercise their faith. Jesus knew that faith and action were mutual terms intertwined and interlocked! They are two inseparable truths. Read what James had to say about this marvelous relationship between faith and works:

> What good is it, my brothers, if someone says
> he has faith, but does not have works? Can his
> faith save him?
> If a brother or sister is without clothes and
> lacks daily food, and one of you says to them,
> "Go in peace, keep warm, and eat well," but
> you don't give them what the body needs, what
> good is it? In the same way faith, if it doesn't
> have works, is dead by itself.

But someone will say, "You have faith,
and I have works." Show me your faith
without works, and I will show faith from
my works. You believe that God is one; you
do well. The demons also believe—and they
shudder.

Foolish man! Are you willing to learn that
faith without works is useless? Wasn't Abraham
our father justified by works when he offered
Isaac his son on the altar? You see that faith
was active together with his works, and by
works, faith was perfected. So the Scripture was
fulfilled that says, Abraham believed God, and
it was credited to him for righteousness, and he
was called God's friend. You see that a man is
justified by works and not by faith alone. And
in the same way, didn't works also justify Rahab
the prostitute also justified by works when she
received the messengers and sent them out by
a different route? For just as the body without
the spirit is dead, so also faith without works is
dead. (James 2:14–26)

This powerful passage of Scripture deals with profound
issues. My intention is not to delve into the depths of
understanding demanded by all that James has to say concerning the importance of faith and works. We know that
God's plan for the redemption of sinful people is based
on faith. Faith alone is the means by which we accept

the Word of God. It is the means by which we confess that Jesus alone is Lord. It is the only means by which we believe in our hearts that God raised Jesus from the dead. But the evidence of that faith is the practice of our action. Faith without works is not faith at all. The proof is in the pudding, so to speak.

Here we find the disciples in the boat, standing firmly on the principles of God and His Word and yet floundering about in their fear. Jesus perhaps was asleep because of the requirements of faith and action. Perhaps the Lord Jesus wanted these men to realize just how important their trust in Him was. Perhaps He needed them to spring into action and actually reach out and shake the Savior to wake Him up. This would enhance their dependency and demonstrate to them just how insecure they were in the boat without the active engagement of their Master.

So many of us operate just like these disciples. The storms of life rock our boats mercilessly at times, and we break into a state of panic and fear. Fear is not some make-believe fabrication that smites people from time to time. It is a real emotion experienced by every person that has ever lived on the face of the earth. As one of our great presidents once said, "The greatest fear is fear itself!" How true this is even in a Christian's life and testimony. Jesus knows all about our troubles.

7. Jesus proved His point before He provided His solution (v. 26). A sequence of events unfolds as the disciples reach out and shake the Lord Jesus from His apparent slumber:

- They reach out to Him.
- They cry out to Him.
- He responds to them.
- He takes action for them.

Perhaps this is something worth making note of. Often we find ourselves looking for instant and quick solutions to our problems. Seemingly, we treat God like some kind of drive-through service. When troubles come our way, we drive up to the window and stick our heads out. We have read the menu and know enough to order what we need or want. Having done so, we proceed to the window where we expect our order to be delivered promptly and exactly according to the specifics of our order. Sometimes we are disgusted when we have to be told to pull up to the curb while our order is being freshly prepared. At other times we become deeply disturbed because something we ordered has been left out of the bag.

God is not a made-to-order service. He is our heavenly Father who loves us more than we can ever imagine. His only desire is to love us, and because this is His only desire, we must remember what real love brings to the table. It involves correction, rebuke, discipline, realignment, direction, solutions, and much teaching. This is exactly what Jesus does when the disciples wake Him up in desperation. I am sure they were not in the mood for a lecture at that particular moment. Their lives were at stake. They must have looked at one another as if to say, "I wish Jesus would save the sermon until later on during the day." Peter most likely would have even huffed and puffed a little, and perhaps Matthew stole a small glance at one of the others. Others might have shrugged their shoulders, and some might have just stared in horrified disbelief that the Lord Jesus would choose such an inopportune time to give them a little talking to about the quality of their faith! They were drowning!

But Jesus never marches according to the drumbeat of man. His ways are not our ways. His timing is not our timing. But one thing is for sure. He knows what is going on. He knows all about our circumstances. He knows how far is far enough. He knows exactly what we need and when we need it. He knows what we need to hear and when we need to hear what we need to hear!

Take another look at this saga as it unfolds in the boat. The disciples are at the point of desperation and they wake Jesus up. And so He gives them a quick sermon! "Why are you so fearful, you of little faith?" Perhaps Jesus knew that this was the moment they would actually listen to what He was saying to them. Again this sounds familiar, does it not?

What I am about to say is not popular, I know, but it is true. Sometimes I truly believe the Lord allows our circumstances to go on because we are not listening, and some never learn. I have known people who seem to have a great propensity to turn to the Lord every time they get into trouble and need Him, but as soon as their overturned boat is turned right side up, they are off to the races again. This is one of the reasons I am so concerned about America.

This is the greatest nation in the world. I believe the Lord has placed His hand on this nation in a special way over the decades of her existence. How many times have we been brought to the brink of disaster or destruction? God's people, and all the rest of the people who claim to be God's people in times of need, flock to church and bend the knee before the Lord. He answers our prayers many times over. I believe He does because God's people pray and God answers prayer! But it does not take too long for many of those same people to take off and do their own thing without any thought of God. Until the next crisis, of course!

Perhaps this was why the Lord Jesus chose this dramatic and urgent moment to share a few things with His boys. They were important to Him, and we know that everything Jesus did on the earth was designed by God to illustrate exactly what He requires of all of us. The key here is the mandate to sit up and take note of what you believe to be true as you place your full faith and trust in Him.

Jesus wanted these men to understand something that was even more important than their healing. He spoke to the issue of faith when He compared faith to a grain of mustard seed:

> He presented another parable to them: "The
> kingdom of heaven is like a mustard seed that
> a man took and sowed in his field. It's the
> smallest of all the seeds, but when grown, it's
> taller than the vegetables and becomes a tree,

so that the birds of the sky come and nest in its
branches." (Matt. 13:31–32)

I have seen mustard seeds in Israel, and they are very
small seeds. The thing about them is just how big a tree
grows when the mustard seed takes root. Palestinian mustard plants are large shrubs that grow as much as fifteen feet
high. They are certainly large enough for birds and other
critters to nest in. The point Jesus was making to His band
of merry men was that their faith was at issue. All they
needed to depend on was their faith, even though they were
in a dire predicament. Faith had all the power necessary to
deliver them completely.

Jesus proved His point before He bailed them out. Are
you listening to all the Lord has to say to you? Or do you
have to have a crisis before God will get your attention?
Have you been so stubborn in your refusal to listen to Him,
or do you need the Lord to give you a good talking to before
He determines the time is right to provide the solution you
need? If you are looking for hope and a future, think on
these things.

8. *Great blessing was received by all (v. 27).* It is always
so much easier to look in the rearview mirror and realize all
the wonderful things the Lord does for us. Needless to say,
we have the benefit of reading about the way in which these
men were delivered by the hand of the Lord. They did not
have this benefit, but they certainly enjoyed their deliverance. They were so blessed by all that had happened to them

that they were "amazed." I love the hymn "I Stand Amazed in the Presence."

> I stand amazed in the presence of Jesus the
>   Nazarene
> And wonder how He could love me
> A sinner condemned, unclean
> How marvelous. Oh how wonderful.
> (Words and music by Charles H. Gabriel)

This resolution carries with it the resolve to stay in the boat. When you decide not to jump ship and stay the course, you find yourself sailing through life's journey on solid principles. The best about all of this is the fact that the Lord Jesus is in the boat with you. Here are the five lessons learned from this resolution:

1. Know that God knows.
2. Storms can suddenly appear.
3. Christians are not exempt from storms.
4. Faith is the key.
5. Make certain you stay in the boat.

I Am Going to Stay the Course

Our previous resolution encouraged us to stay in the boat. In a symbolic way, the boat is the vehicle in which we are transported through life. We turn our attention now to the things we do in life. One of my favorite stories concerns the famous traveling evangelist, Luther Rice. God used him in so many ways, and he was a blessing to thousands of people during his life. On his deathbed, he apparently commented that God had given him a horse and a spirit, and that he had killed the horse. By "horse" he was referring to his body. This was the vehicle God had given him to carry out all the duties and responsibilities he had undertaken for the Lord. In reality, Rice's "horse" can be compared to the boat of the previous discussion. The "course" is the work we do.

In his final public speech to Israel, Samuel spoke of his own journey of life. He outlined the significance of staying the course and remaining true to all that the Lord had called him to do. This is one of the most action-packed speeches in the entire Bible. It is a living testimony to a life well lived and to a man who was faithful to the end despite the many hardships and challenges he faced. But he stayed the course! This is a long passage, but it must be read in its entirety if we are to grasp fully the extent to which this man stayed the course.

> Then Samuel said to all Israel, "I have carefully listened to everything you have said to me and placed a king over you. But now, you can see that the king is leading you. As for me, I'm old and gray, and my sons are here with you. I have led you from my youth until today. Here I am. Bring charges against me before the LORD and His anointed: Whose ox or donkey have

I taken? Whom have I wronged or mistreated? From whose hand have I taken a bribe to overlook something? I will return it to you."

"You haven't wronged us, you haven't mistreated us, and you haven't taken anything from anyone's hand," they responded.

He said to them, "The LORD is a witness against you, and His anointed is a witness today that you haven't found anything in my hand."

"He is a witness," they said.

The Samuel said to the people, "The LORD who appointed Moses and Aaron and who brought your ancestors up from the land of Egypt, is a witness. Now present yourselves, so I may judge you before the LORD about all your righteous acts He has done for you and your ancestors." . . .

"Now, therefore, present yourselves and see this great thing that the LORD will do before your eyes. Isn't the wheat harvest today? I will call on the LORD and He will send thunder and rain, so that you will know and see what a great evil you committed in the LORD's sight by requesting a king for yourselves." Samuel called on the LORD, and on that day the LORD sent thunder and rain. As a result, all the people feared the LORD and Samuel.

They pleaded with Samuel, "Pray to the LORD your God for your servants, so we won't die! For we have added to all our sins the evil of requesting a king for ourselves."

Samuel replied, "Don't be afraid. Even though you have committed all this evil, don't turn away from following the LORD. Instead, worship the LORD with all your heart. Don't turn away to follow worthless things that can't profit or deliver you; they are worthless. The LORD will not abandon His people, because of His great name and because He has determined to make you His own people.

"As for me, I vow that I will not sin against the LORD by ceasing to pray for you. I will teach you the good and right way. Above all, fear the LORD and worship Him faithfully with all your heart, considering the great things He has done for you. However, if you continue to do what is evil, both you and your king will be swept away." (1 Sam. 12:1–7, 16–25)

Any study of the life and times of Samuel will leave no doubt as to the adventures he encountered. God had raised him up for his day and age, and he had responded to the challenge. Samuel erected six signposts for us at the end of his life. Each one carries a special injunction to stay the course and keep on keeping on.

1. Accept your role in life (v. 2). Samuel had no hesitation in saying that his role had been to lead them from the time of his youth. This is what the Lord God had called him to be and to do. He heard that call, he knew what was expected of him, and he stayed the course. I often have had the privilege of teaching groups of young pastors and ministers. I cannot think of a higher privilege. There are many times when the subject centers on personal issues. One of the outlines I use focuses on several important issues in life.

- The issue of one's conversion
- The issue of one's call
- The issue of one's commitment

Once you have established and settled the fact of your salvation in Christ, it is vital to establish the fact of your call to serve the Lord. I do not believe the call to serve God in a full-time capacity is a choice people make. It's not like God lines up several options and says, "Now let's see, you have the choice of becoming a doctor, or a nurse, or a teacher, or a mechanic, or a missionary, or a preacher!" Not at all! The call to serve the Lord Jesus as a full-time vocation is decisive and distinctive. He either calls you, or He does not! If you and I cannot or will not accept the role and accompanying responsibility of that role to serve the Lord Jesus, then we may as well go back and become the President of the United States of America, if that is all we can do! Samuel stayed the course through thick and through thin because he accepted his role in life.

2. Guard your personal integrity (vv. 3–5). No doubt about Samuel at this point. Can you just imagine looking all the people square in the eyes and challenging them to lay any blame for anything at his feet? His integrity was totally intact. Someone has said that your integrity is all you have. This is so true. I am certain millions of parents have implored their sons and daughters to keep their integrity intact. These people could not find one single thing to place at his feet that would in any way discredit his witness for God. This may perhaps be the source of your discouragement. You can be restored if you are willing to confess your sins to the Lord Jesus. Remember He is the faithful one who will forgive your sins and cleanse you (1 John 1:9).

3. Listen to godly advice (v. 14). Samuel stood before the people even in his old age and gave them advice. Evidently they were willing to listen to him. It seems to me this is a signpost on the highway to staying the course. The Lord has placed so many people at our disposal. I only have to think about my wife, Karyn, when it comes to this issue. She is my constant source of godly advice.

I do not know where I would be or how I would be able to lead my church to be on mission for the Lord if not for the numbers of godly people in our church. It is essential to listen to them and to value what the Lord has to say through them. This is a sure antidote to discouragement. Make it your business to surround yourself with godly people. Go after them. Seek them out. They are everywhere. Pray about this important matter and watch what the Lord does. He will bring them to you, and they will bless your lives in ways you cannot even imagine or comprehend.

4. Unclutter your life (v. 16). I love this point because it is one of the most seriously relevant points to make for all of us. Many people who have a diminished perspective of the future are people who suffer from clutter. Their lives are so overloaded they cannot see anything but their own situations and circumstances. Look at what Samuel said to the people. He stressed the fact that the Lord was about to show them great and mighty things. These things would be paraded before their eyes. But what good would that be if they could not see what was going on?

Perhaps this is one of the great scourges of our lives today. Just think about the Lord's Day, for example. God told us to remember the Lord's day and to set it aside to worship Him. This was all well in days gone by when life was conducted at a much slower pace and when Sundays were protected. Today it has simply become another day in the week. School kids become seriously jeopardized in their athletic endeavors, practices are often held on the Lord's day, and every kind of sport is played without regard for worship. Yet it gets worse. Many people arrive in church each Sunday unprepared to worship. So many things are going on, and they have so many places to be and so many people to visit and so many shops to peruse that church is simply pushed into the background. The result is that many people sit in the pews with cluttered minds. Their thoughts and hearts are elsewhere. It follows that it is all the more difficult to place yourself in a position to hear what God is saying, let alone do what God is saying.

Now I am no exception to this challenge. I desperately need to hear from the Lord because He is my primary strength and encourager. But it is so difficult to see Him at work when my mind is so cluttered with everything else. Perhaps you may need to reevaluate your life and reorder some priorities.

5. Stand in awe of the Lord (v. 18). Most of us lack the proper reverence for the Lord Jesus. Even when we see Him do great and wonderful things for us, we soon forget and move on. To me this matter of standing in awe of God speaks to an attitude of worship and thanksgiving. Remember the ten lepers Jesus told us about. He healed all of them, and only one of them came back to say thank you. Are we any different when it comes to the hand of the Lord on our lives? We often pray for miracles, but we seldom stand in awe when God sends them our way. We often pray and ask the Lord to bless our children, but when He does, we resort to silence. We often see God do great and mighty things before our eyes, but we seldom hold high His name before the people.

I really think this is one of the reasons so many people struggle. It is a spirit of ingratitude. We have a casual attitude to the Lord after He has stood in the bow of the boat and calmed the storms of our lives. Perhaps the Lord does not take too kindly to this.

Samuel's action left no doubt in the people's minds as to who was God. They had presented their case, and God's man had directed them. No matter how wrong they had been, Samuel still told them to stay the course. And then, to top it all, he still called on the name of the Lord to manifest

Himself to the people, and God answered his request. It rained cats and dogs to the point that the people stood in awe in His presence and thanked the Lord for the man of God as well.

6. Be compassionate to others (v. 20). This is another one of those things in the Bible that blesses my heart and challenges me to the core. Here we find the people scared to death for good reason. They had disobeyed the Lord and had refused to listen to God's anointed servant. Samuel had begged God to overlook their disobedience and stood in the gap for the people he loved. He did not forget his role. With their eyes opened, they saw God act in a decisive and unapologetic way. Fear gripped their hearts because they realized in a fresh way that God was not someone to be messed with or treated lightly. In their minds it was over. They knew the Lord would not tolerate their antics. They knew their hand had been called and that, more than likely, God would kill them all. But Samuel acted with great compassion.

Compassion is the hallmark of God's grace. It is easy to talk about and even easier to preach about, but it is so difficult to do. People can be total jerks in their attitudes and behavior toward one another. People can be so unkind and can assassinate another in a heartbeat! In the local church, tongues can wag at a hundred miles an hour. Others who spend hours on the phone doing nothing but sharing all the local gossip in town destroy many people's lives. It's time to face the facts. And so much of this goes on inside the church of the living God and is done by people who should know better!

Now let's get back to compassion. You may wonder if I think it is easy to be compassionate. Not at all! Even Samuel probably would have liked to have seen a few heads roll! But God expects compassion from us. One of the reasons we struggle is because we are not compassionate. I do not believe we can stay the course if we are not compassionate even to those who deserve it least. I am so glad the Lord Jesus was compassionate to me. He hung on that cruel cross and asked the Father to forgive me because I was numbered among all those who knew not what we were doing. Not one of us deserves the love and compassion of the Lord Jesus. But He went to the cross willingly and in full and complete obedience to the Father.

Every time you exercise compassion your spiritual temperature will rise. You will find a new reason to be hopeful, and a fresh wind will blow through your life. And if you cannot find it in yourself to be compassionate, go out and do something compassionate.

Perhaps one of the highlights of my life has been to be the guest of my friend Phil Waldrep. Many years ago the Lord Jesus put it on his heart to travel to New England and begin a retreat for pastors and their wives, who would come from all over the region. On one such encouragement retreat, I do not believe those precious people could have had any idea just how much they blessed my life. These men and women are on the front line of service for the Lord. They are choice servants of God. Many of them serve in small situations, and many of them have to work long and arduous hours to provide for their families. They have a cheer and joy about them that is so refreshing and uplifting. Phil asked me to join him in Vermont to share the Word of God with them. I came away with my cup filled to overflowing.

To be honest, I went to Vermont with an open heart and the right attitude. Nothing gives me greater joy than to minister to men and women who are so devoted to the cause of Christ. They know their role in life, and many have stuck to it.

One couple I met really blessed me. John and Joanne Tracy serve the Barre Baptist Fellowship in Washington, Vermont. They had been there for nineteen years by the time I met them. Their story is remarkable. Joanne had married at a fairly young age. The abuse she was subject to was horrific. Her husband drank alcohol day and night. He frequently beat her up, and she became the victim of unbelievable abuse. Many nights found her looking after the children at pubs while they watched their daddy get drunk. When she was pregnant with her third child, her husband severely beat her up again and then had her small children jump up and down on her abdomen. She lost the baby and somehow found the resolve to walk out and away from him. Almost destitute, she began a new life in the town of her parents while living under extreme duress and embarrassment. People snubbed her, and she was often told the abuse and rapes had all been her fault.

Then she met a wonderful, compassionate man by the name of Louis J. Tracy. He went by the name of John. Jesus

Christ entered her life, and the transformation had begun. Nineteen years previous to my meeting them, they had begun a ministry to down-and-out people in the Washington community. John Tracy was called to be interim pastor, and the Washington Baptist Church adopted the Barre Baptist Fellowship. In November 1989, John started weekly services at the Cedar Brook Care Home in lower Graniteville. They had eleven residents and in three years baptized six people. By January 1991, the church had called John as full-time pastor.

On December 1997, a soup kitchen called Open Door Fellowship was opened with $10 in the food fund and accompanied by some borrowed pots and pans and many prayers. The first month averaged seventeen people per meal, and this rapidly increased to about thirty-seven per meal. God even provided a house for them, which they were able to buy for $35 thousand.

The Tracys continue to honor the Lord with unbelievable servants' hearts. What really harnessed my attention was the fact that they have never received a salary from their work. These two saints of the Lord live only on their social security checks. In 2008 their total offerings from the church were $3,000. Of this amount they still gave 25 percent to missions, as if they are not a mission themselves!

While in Vermont, God did some wonderful things in my life. I went with a good attitude and a ready heart to serve the Lord, and He gave it all back to me a thousandfold!

As we come to the end of this book on overcoming discouragement, I pray that God will use the lives of people like Nehemiah, Samuel, Moses, and modern-day people like the Tracys, Billy Graham, and even the life of one like Don Wilton to inspire your life and future. All of these people have overcome discouragement in their lives at one point or another and had or have a bright future. God wants the same for your life and future. He has a plan for your life, my friend. Do not let the circumstances of a fallen world throw you into a downward spiral. Look up! He is there with open arms. His Word is sharp and applicable to your life as a man or woman in the world today. I encourage you to keep this book close and in times of discouragement go back and look at places you have marked. Go back and look at the verses you have marked in the Bible as sources of encouragement.

Be encouraged! Never give up . . . never give up . . . never give up!